Mysteries of Love and Grief

Frieda and Ira embracing, 1925.

The whole family, just prior to Ira's death.

Mysteries of Love and Grief

reflections on a plainswoman's life

sandra scofield

texas tech university press

This book is typeset in Scala Sans. The paper used in this book meets the minimum requirements of ANSI/NISO Z39.48-1992 (R1997). ∞

Designed by Kasey McBeath
Cover photograph from author's collection

Library of Congress Cataloging-in-Publication Data
Scofield, Sandra Jean, 1943–
Mysteries of love and grief : reflections on a plainswoman's life / Sandra Scofield.
pages cm
ISBN 978-0-89672-941-4 (hardback : alkaline paper) – ISBN 978-0-89672-942-1 (e-book) 1. Hambleton, Frieda Katherine Harms, 1906–1983. 2. Scofield, Sandra Jean, 1943 —Childhood and youth. 3. Scofield, Sandra Jean, 1943— Family. 4. Women pioneers–High Plains (U.S.)–Biography. 5. Working mothers–High Plains (U.S.)–Biography. 6. Widows–High Plains (U.S.)–Biography. 7. Grand-mothers–High Plains (U.S.)–Biography. 8. High Plains (U.S.)–Social life and customs–20th century. 9. Devol (Okla.)–Biography. 10. Wichita Falls (Tex.)–Biography. I. Title.
F595.H29S36 2015
920.70979'0904—dc23

2015012803

15 16 17 18 19 20 21 22 23 / 9 8 7 6 5 4 3 2 1

Texas Tech University Press
Box 41037 | Lubbock, Texas 79409-1037 USA
800.832.4042 | ttup@ttu.edu | www.ttupress.org

Dedication:
For my kin

CONTENTS

ACKNOWLEDGMENTS

I am grateful to my daughter, Jessica, and my cousin Rebecca for their research. To my Aunt Mae for a lifetime of stories. And to Judith Keeling, with whom I finally found the will to write about my grandmother.

Frieda Katherine Harms Hambleton

Born: January 20, 1906, Alva, Indian Territory*
Died: September 18, 1983, Wichita Falls, Texas
Buried: Devol, Oklahoma

Husband: Ira Arcadius Hambleton
Born: February 28, 1904, Temple, Oklahoma Territory
Died: September 26, 1936, Chickasha, Oklahoma
Buried: Chickasha, Oklahoma

Children: Edith Aileen (1925–1959), Eula Mae (1926–),
Louis Edward (1930–2001)

*This would become part of Oklahoma, along with Oklahoma Territory, when it was admitted to statehood in November 1907. In the 1940 census taken in Arizona, Frieda was listed as "American Citizen Born Abroad."

AN ABBREVIATED FAMILY TREE FOR FRIEDA

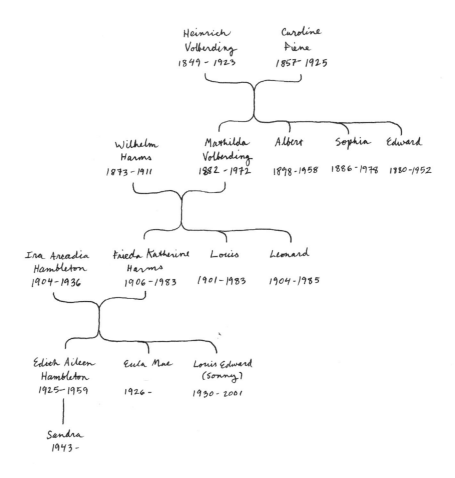

Heinrich
Volberding
1849 - 1923

Caroline
Fiene
1857 - 1925

Wilhelm
Harms
1873 - 1911

Mathilda
Volberding
1882 - 1972

Albert
1898 - 1958

Sophia
1886 - 1978

Edward
1880 - 1952

Ira Arcadia
Hambleton
1904 - 1936

Frieda Katherine
Harms
1906 - 1983

Louis
1901 - 1983

Leonard
1904 - 1985

Edith Aileen
Hambleton
1925 - 1959

Eula Mae
1926 -

Louis Edward
(Sonny)
1930 - 2001

Sandra
1943 -

THE STORY TEST

For years I had been a weekend writer, and my stories had almost always arisen from recollections of my young adulthood when I wandered and bumped up against the consequences of traveling without direction. Then, a few years before my grandmother Frieda died in 1983, I began writing about my family. I wanted to tell stories about my childhood. I don't know why. It might have been as simple as not having any other ideas. One year I taught, and then the next year I didn't, so I spent a lot of time reading and writing; then I taught again, and then I didn't; then my grandmother died, and I went back to writing and made that my job.

I didn't know what I was doing. I hadn't studied writing; I didn't know anyone who could advise me. I had always read a lot, so I imagined myself interrogating writers, and I imagined their answers, and those were my guides. When the dream inside you is as vivid as the one you are living, when there is no one to answer the questions that plague you, and your melancholy feels like a chasm, it is thrilling to discover that stories fill you up.

I believe that everyone has a complex interior life, and I decided early on that writing would be a way for me to honor that attribute in myself and in other people. I have never truly understood my characters until I've told their stories; essentially, they reveal themselves to me. It was a while before I wondered if I might understand my loved ones better by doing the same thing.

Frieda read one of my stories—a long one, seventy pages or so—in the spring of the year before she died. It was about the summer when I was nine, when my mother, daddy, little sister, and I went to Ohio in an old car to visit Daddy's family. There was a tangle of stories in those pages, and mystery, too, mystery being one of the stories, and the trip was the container for all of them. The mystery began and ended with my grandmother, who wasn't on the trip and might have been left out of the story completely except for the money she had given me to take, just in case we needed it.

When I began to write about that summer, I didn't have any doubts about my memories. Since I was a child, I've narrated my life to myself, like a reporter. I thought of myself as writing fiction, but that didn't mean it wasn't true. I remember the afternoons in the basement of the farmhouse in Barnesville, where my mother and I read old women's magazines, escaping the sultry heat and the cold-hearted family; we snuggled on a daybed that smelled of mildew and wondered when someone would come looking for us, but nobody ever did. And I remember Daddy's sister's house outside Washington, DC, where it was even hotter and wetter and more miserable than Ohio. His sister's husband, a highway patrolman, looked at my mother with a nasty smirk, and when he saw me watching him, he turned his ugly glare on me. My mother and I didn't like any of Daddy's family, and I guess they didn't like us, either, though they doted on my little sister and, of course, on Daddy, who was jovial and relaxed in a way I had never seen him be at home, where we had lived in my grandmother's house until that very summer when I was nine and we moved into a place of our own, when we went to Ohio and a dirty old uncle leered at my mother. I couldn't think how to explain it all to my grandmother when we got home, so what I said was, their houses all have stairs and basements.

I could remember, while typing out my story, how I had wondered what my grandmother would have thought if she had known back then what was going on in Ohio. I thought she would have said she was sorry I had to go. She had been upset with my mother for working two months as a carhop at the Pig Stand Drive-In to get the money for the trip, and I knew she worried about Mother's health all the time we were away. And she had warned me that Daddy's folks might not like me, though she didn't say why.

And all the while her little change purse with the rolled up bills in it was in a pouch in my cardboard suitcase, and a good thing it was, because of course we did need it on the way home when the car broke down.

As I wrote about that long ago summer, I wished I had told my grandmother that there were things about the trip that were fun—the coming and going, seeing sights, making our lunches in the car, reading Burma Shave signs. We went to Mammoth Caves, and we saw a two-headed calf. I wished I had told her that even though my mother and I had felt unwelcome in Ohio, we hadn't cared, because the Yankees didn't matter to us, and we knew we would go home. The way I thought as an adult about being nine years old on a trip to see strangers didn't fit my story, though, and so I didn't say those mitigating things in 1982, even though they had come to mind, and I could have mentioned them in my letter that accompanied the manuscript to my grandmother. I must have thought that if I amended the experience, I would spoil the effect of the narrative in which a child is baffled by the way grownups treat her and each other. I must have wanted my grandmother to feel some of what I had felt when I was away from seeing her or talking to her for the first time ever except once when I was too little to remember. And I wanted her to know that the money she gave me, the money we needed somewhere near Oklahoma City to fix the car, had made my mother furious, and she had told me, standing on the road by the open trunk of the car, that my grandmother would be very sorry that she used me to get back at her. Because that had been the most perplexing thing of all, that a person could see someone's help as hateful and that there were sides in a tug of war, and I was the rope being pulled between them.

I remember taking the manuscript to the post office and after I had mailed it, standing on the sidewalk in the sunshine and thinking about how much I had filtered my life through what I thought of as my grandmother's worries about my mother and me, but I wasn't experienced enough as a writer to understand that that was the real story.

***

She wrote in a letter, among other things, that she had read my interesting story and that she wondered if my sister thought about family too. It certainly wasn't the reaction I might have hoped for, but I don't remember being upset. I thought she didn't know what to say, and what really mattered to me was that she had read my story at all.

She also wrote that my mother had minded that we—my grandmother and I—were so close. That was the most she had said about my mother in all the years since she died. I don't know why I didn't sit down and pour my heart out to her right then and there and say: yes, it's true about you and me, and I'm glad and I'll never forget. Maybe she would have poured her heart out, too. Maybe she wanted to, and I just needed to ask.

Wasn't I trying to be a writer? I could have typed a long letter. I could have said, when we moved out of your house, I felt like a rubber band being stretched to break. I loved you both, you and my mother, and I know you both loved me, but I thought I was guilty of something, or someone was; surely there was something I didn't know that made my mother want to keep me away from you. I learned early on that we were all keeping secrets, even me, who didn't know what the secrets were but who didn't ask and so joined the conspiracy that silence always is.

If I had finally said something to her about our history and our love, it would have had to have been in a letter. I was in Jacksonville, Oregon, and she was in Wichita Falls, Texas, and I didn't go to see her that year. We talked often on the phone, but we talked about the weather and how my daughter was getting to be such a big girl. We had never talked about our feelings, but she had given me an opening in her letter, and I could have answered her in a way that let her know I cherished her. I can't say why I didn't. I feel sodden with regret. It was a kind of arrogance, thinking that I could say something better if I made it up than I could if I said it straight out. Over Christmas break—I was teaching second grade—I started a story about the year I was in seventh grade, when Daddy got a job in the oil fields and my sister and our mother went to West Texas to live with him, while I stayed with the Sisters at my school, and my mother said I couldn't go to my grandmother's house, not even for one weekend, all that year. I could have talked to my grandmother about that year when we had been separated as if she had a restraining order. I have a photograph of the two of us taken that spring by a stranger who had been kind enough to snap us with my grandmother's camera while we sat huddled on a picnic table. My grandmother's arm is around my waist. I wonder what the stranger thought, looking through the viewfinder at two miserable human beings who for some reason wanted a picture. We would not have explained that I had slipped away from the school grounds to meet my grandmother for a few minutes before she went to her four-to-twelve shift at General Mills, packing flour. I had said, shortly before the picture was taken, *what's wrong with her!* because there was no reason for my mother to control my life all the way from Odessa just to make a point my grandmother already understood. My grandmother put her finger on my lips and shook her head. *She has the say;* that was what she always told me. You might think that our expressions of frustration and resentment spoil the photograph, but to me they capture the fierce love my grandmother and I felt for each other and the way that the loneliness of my isolation, which I tried to see in romantic terms, was eating away my capacity for affection and intimacy.

I didn't have the photograph when I started my story in 1982, but I remembered that day or one like it, for there were many days that my grandmother found a way to see me, if only for a few moments. She came to the school block during my lunch hour when she wasn't working days, and I ran to the chain link fence to clasp her hands. We hugged like lovers at the periphery of a prison camp. Truly, I liked being with the Sisters, I liked school and going to daily Mass, and maybe I liked the feeling of orphanhood, too, because it dramatized what I felt: that I was condemned to be without a mother, and if I could do nothing about it—not even understand it—then I could at least fall into the pathos of it. Even then, I was telling myself my story.

Maybe in 1982 I thought that a story about that time would have a power that a letter wouldn't. Maybe I thought my grandmother would be touched that I would write a story about how much I had wanted to be with her. Maybe I thought the story would bring up old shared pain—another way for us to clutch over the fence—without having to actually talk about it.

And maybe I was wallowing in a pond of nostalgia and self-pity, and my impulse was to find a *good reason* for my feelings and then to tell the world what had happened to me. I had written many stories in my life, and I had hardly cared at all whether anyone read them; the point was to *think* them, to *feel* them. This new story brought up new ideas about what writing was for. You could say that Frieda became for me not just my grandmother but a reader. She would be the story's test case, and I felt myself stepping back from what I had written, wondering how to judge its effect. I knew what it meant to me, but how would Frieda feel? And more thrillingly, what would a stranger feel? I read the pages I had written, and I decided to start all over again, because I knew that having a reason for the story—and being able to say what it was—meant I could write it better.

But teaching second grade is exhausting, and then coming home to make supper and be with my daughter and my husband, and laundry, and migraines too many to count. So the story lay on my chipboard table in the bedroom month after month, and then my grandmother had a heart attack in May while visiting my aunt in Lubbock, and when I went to see her she didn't want to talk. All summer I tried to finish the story and didn't, and I never did; in September, she died.

Frieda died in her house on Grant Street in Wichita Falls, Texas, on September 18, 1983. A neighbor who checked in on her every day found her. It was a Sunday.

We had just finished supper, and I had cleared the table. I was standing right by the wall-mounted phone when my aunt's husband called to tell me. As soon as I heard his voice—he certainly had never called my house before—I knew why he had called, and I hung up and sat down on the floor and pushed my face hard against my knees. I thought of my aunt, maybe hunched over at the kitchen table or flung across her bed, and I resented her for sending me the news by way of her ugly, stupid husband.

My husband was loading the dishwasher. He wiped his hands and came and knelt beside me, but before he could say anything, I pushed him away.

I didn't want comfort; I wouldn't be comforted; there was no such thing as comfort.

I didn't go to Texas for the funeral. I called the convent in Wichita Falls and spoke to one of the Sisters and asked if someone would go to the funeral home in my stead, see my grandmother, and say a prayer. This might seem odd to some people, but one of the Sisters did go. She wrote me to say that my grandmother looked peaceful and very dear and that she had prayed to thank God for my grandmother's life and to ask Him to remember me because she knew that it would be hard for me to be without her.

There were good reasons for me not to go. Frieda had not wanted me to come and be with her during the summer after her heart attack when she was alive, and we all knew what was coming, so what was the good now? I hadn't been to a funeral since my mother died in 1959. I didn't have a job, and we were on a tight budget, living on my husband's salary as a high school English teacher in a poor school district. And I didn't want to be with the family. I wanted my grief to be mine alone.

A few months later, my Aunt Mae sent me a couple of boxes packed with things she had taken from the house. She told me they held Frieda's Bible, which she had had since she married in 1924, and also letters, photographs, my grandmother's baptism certificate and nurse's cap, and a few other documents. I made a place for them in the bottom of our kitchen pantry. I told myself I would look at everything as soon as I could.

It was many years before I examined their contents. Maybe a year at a time would go by that I didn't think of the boxes, and then I would. I'd open the cupboard doors and stand there looking at the boxes as if they might crawl out and speak to me, but at most I would skim a letter or look at a few photographs. At last I felt compelled, called, if you will, by letters brittle and brown with age, black-and-white photographs, social security cards, and poems from newspapers, copied by my grandmother into her Bible—sentimental verses meant to calm a grieving heart. I opened them one night when only I was awake, and I was still at it in the morning when my husband came into the kitchen to make his breakfast.

I knew I would write a story about my grandmother's life, though not just yet. I certainly didn't expect to be an old woman before I undertook the task, but it seems to have taken that long for me to understand that my grandmother had her own story and that it was her story that I wanted to tell. It wasn't until I began the writing that I understood that she had taken her story with her.

I still love her as a child does; as I did. She has ever been the extension of me that children feel their mothers are. I grew up in her house. I came home to her when I needed to. And though I don't want to set aside those feelings I have for her—the sensibility of a child—I want also to love her for herself. I want to say: Here is a woman. Here is what I know about her life. She spoke German as a child. She lived in Oklahoma and New Mexico and Arizona and Texas, on tenant farms and in a settler's cabin, in boxcars and stucco houses. She labored her whole life. She married four times, but she loved only the husband of her youth. She suffered tragic losses and still got up in the morning. She cultivated a garden and apricot trees. She took care of a dying daughter, and later, her dying mother. She took care of me. She became a nurse at fifty-five and later yet learned to paint. In her last year, she made quilt tops for her granddaughters. She once had a dachshund called Tiny.

All I can do is my best. Like a mourner at a grave, I honor her. If I had the skill, I would paint her portrait. I would paint her standing in her backyard, her hand shading her eyes as she studies the sky, watching the storm come in.

WHAT WAS LEFT BEHIND

DISTRIBUTION

Frieda's will divided everything equally among her three children: her son, Louis ("Sonny"), her daughter Eula Mae, and her dead daughter Edith's share allotted to my sister Karen and me. Though the will was boilerplate and scrupulously fair, Sonny protested it, saying that his sister had influenced Frieda.

There was little to divide. The house, built in 1953, was on a street of modest homes, some dilapidated, almost none with garages; many, like Frieda's, without driveways at all. It, too, was a humble house, though during the short term of her last marriage, Frieda had added a large room across the back, and for the first time in her life, she had been able to do laundry at home. Her husband was legally blind, but he had building experience, and he was able to instruct and guide her as she added the extension without a contractor, working alongside the day laborers, doing everything from framing to sheetrocking and painting and laying linoleum. Her brother Len, a licensed electrician, wired the room. It had baseboard heaters, safer and more effective than the single open-flame gas heater she used in the living room. It had a bathroom. It was a space where a family could put a television and couch, a table, and chairs. That room probably created most of the value of the house when it sold. The house had been cramped and basic; it had once flooded, and a fire had destroyed the living room. But now you went in the house and right through the kitchen to the spacious back room.

Other than the house, Frieda only had a few hundred dollars in the bank and some old, basically worthless furniture. Little as there was, it was sad to squander it on the cost of a quarrel. My uncle's lawyer soon dropped him because he wouldn't be reasonable. After a while, my aunt and I tried to give him the house, but he wouldn't even agree to that. He had vaulted from Frieda's death straight into a wild anger he wouldn't (or couldn't) explain. (It got much worse: divorce, heart attacks, estrangement from his children, right to his death.) His behavior was a perfect example of successful anarchy, in which there is no purpose in mayhem except to disrupt order. Nothing went as Frieda had planned. Sonny's own children, whose names were taped on the best of the furniture from our great-grandmother's farm, lost their legacy. Everything that had value in Frieda's house was sold at auction from her front yard. The court-appointed executor filled a few boxes with items that had no commercial value, and my aunt picked them up. Sad thing, a fuss like this, he told her. He said, the day won't come that I'll sell a family Bible.

Someone bought my mother's dishes, a pretty set, white with tiny flowers. Frieda had saved them for me, and I had promised, year after year, to come and get them. It must have hurt her feelings terribly that I didn't, but I am sure she assumed I would get them at last when she died.

When I finally sorted photographs from the box my aunt had sent, I mailed some to my sister in Connecticut. In one, she is holding a fish she had caught; I remember that day at Balmorhea, a beautiful natural spring pool in West Texas, where Daddy had taken us camping. In another picture she is at the top of a slide; I think it is a picture from our trip to Ohio, when we stopped at a city park in St. Louis. There are snapshots of us in Easter outfits, others from a birthday party for my sister. I made a copy for her of my favorite—four of us cousins in front of Aunt Mae's and Uncle Howard's tiny Halliburton company-owned house in Kermit, Texas, standing stiffly formal, as if we sensed that we were making a record for posterity.

My sister sent me word through Mae that she had thrown the photographs away. She is angry, like Sonny, I guess, and if she knows why, she doesn't say. I remind myself that she was not quite twelve years old when our mother died. I am sorry now that we were split up, me to Frieda, my sister to our aunt. It seemed logical at the time; her cousin Joan was her same age and they were close. Mae's house was a family environment. There was never a question that I wanted to be with my grandmother. The worst mistake was my sister's own doing; after a few years she went to live with her daddy and his wife, a woman who found adolescence contemptible. Of course our mother would never be mentioned to Karen again; Edith would fade into a ghost of the woman who abandoned her. And Frieda would forever be (unfairly) the grandmother who chose Sandra, and not Karen.

Mysteries of grace and grief

We loved her, and we knew that she loved us. There were hundreds of trips back and forth from Wichita Falls to towns in West Texas where my aunt lived, and later where my family lived. There were summer excursions to fish and swim and camp and water-ski, sometimes as far as the Wichita Mountains near Lawton, Oklahoma. There were picnics in parks and birthday parties and Christmas trees and innumerable trips to Frieda's mother's and stepfather's farm in Devol, Oklahoma.

The family was always getting together. One year there was a picnic in a park for my birthday (August 5). It was near my grandmother's house. My uncle and his kids were with us; Mae and her kids were there. We had all gathered a little after three o'clock and were waiting for Frieda to show up after work. She appeared after five, looking flustered and breathless. She had been stopped on Kell Boulevard and fined for speeding, even though she explained that she was hurrying from work to a party for a seven-year-old. She was so mad that when she got in the car she shifted into the wrong gear and backed into the cop car, which got her a second summons and the promise of a bill for damage to the bumper.

My mother hugged Frieda and started to cry. Sonny started laughing and said, it was a durned good thing she didn't run the poor guy down.

It was one time I remember for sure that nobody got mad at anybody and we all went home stuffed and tired and happy. I got a little plastic flute as a present, and I had it as late as 1965, when I last lived with my grandmother, but all I ever could do was blow a few shrill notes and wonder what it was that Sonny thought was so funny.

* * *

She worked in a flour mill more than twenty years, packing sacks in a huge building that was scorching in the summer and frigid in the winter. It looked like a stack of concrete toilet paper rolls. Sometimes I heard her talk on the phone about "that s.o.b.," someone in management. I never heard her complain about the hard labor, the constant drudgery, the stress of rotating shifts. She walked in the door after a shift and had something to drink—a glass of iced tea or maybe milk with crushed crackers stirred in—and then she took a bath. Head to toe, she was covered with flour. She worked in nursing homes, too, and she said the charge nurses were lazy. She loved apple pie and brown beans, and Bishop Sheen and Jack Paar and Johnny Carson. She drove Studebakers for as long as I could remember, until the seventies, when she drove a Chevrolet.

Wherever I was, as long as she lived, whatever I was doing, whether she would approve or not, whenever I needed to know I wasn't alone in the world, I knew she loved me. I couldn't say those things about my mother, because she was absorbed in her illness, though she did everything she could to give me a good education and a sense of possibility. My mother's death set me on a long detour away from maturation. My grandmother, though, was always there. When she died, at the natural and reasonable age of seventy-seven, I was knocked to my knees, for they were both gone, and I was at last truly a motherless child.

She was a fiercely loyal matriarch, withholding of what she was feeling but generous with what she thought you needed. She was suspicious of outsiders—bosses, creditors, politicians, salesmen, preachers—and she made me think I couldn't trust anyone except family, when you could tell she thought everyone in the family did wrong things without even trying.

She was angry: thin lips, shoulders tight, hard steps as she walked away. I used to think, why is she so mad? I knew her sorrows—her father dead before she had even started school; her husband dead when she was thirty; my mother sick so long and gone at thirty-three. I knew there was grief in the house long before I knew what it was for. And yes, grief sometimes turns to anger, but how does it turn into a person's engine? What else happened, and who was to blame?

My aunt and I have shaken this old quilt a hundred times: what was the quarrel? Remember the time—? Neither of us can come up with an honest to goodness answer to the question I keep asking: why? My aunt lets things go; she doesn't hold grudges. The best way not to be bitter, she says, is just to forget. (And isn't she the very fountain of memory for me? She's the last one standing, and I can tell you, she isn't bitter, but it isn't because she forgets.)

Pictures go through my mind like a slide show. I remember once we were in Frieda's house on Grant Street. I was in the kitchen buttering bread when I heard my mother screeching, get in here, Sandra, right this minute! Out the door we all went. Mother shoved my sister and me into the car; Daddy was the driver, and there was Frieda, hitting at Daddy through the open car window beside him. We backed away out of her yard, and it was me screaming until my mother turned around and slapped me. I remember Daddy saying, that's it, Edith, that's it. I doubt he ever spoke another word to Frieda that wasn't business about me. At Mother's funeral, he kept my sister and me in a pew across the aisle from her; at the grave we stood out of the line of her sight. It was awful. That's it, he had said, and he meant it. The lucky thing is, once he'd made his point, he didn't feel enough spite to keep me from her.

I remember a time when Sonny was shouting and Frieda picked up her purse from the couch and walked out of her own house. I remember my mother, stepping out onto the sidewalk to talk to her mother, not letting her inside the house. I was a phantom presence, nothing to do with the quarrels, but I always felt stricken and afraid.

I ask my aunt at least once a year. What was it all about?

She laughs and says, she didn't like our husbands. And though I am at a loss to think of anything specific that happened to set off the whirlwinds of bad feelings, I do think that most fights were over men.

I think Frieda's disapproval always had to do with fear. She could see how things were going to fall through, how undependable husbands were, what trouble lay ahead, but it wasn't her place to say so. Her daughters were defensive about their men; her son was defensive about his failures. And I, motherless, fatherless, grew into my young adulthood feeling entitled to do whatever the hell I wanted.

In May 1983, Frieda had open-heart surgery in Lubbock, Texas, where my aunt lived. I flew there from Oregon two days later. She looked better than I expected, but she was mad that they had operated on her; she hadn't been conscious to make a decision for herself, and she thought Mae should have known she wouldn't want the pain and expense of her surgery. She had to wear long compression socks, and Mae's husband had to help her put them on and pull them up, and I knew she was humiliated by this, not because she was shy, but because she was contemptuous of him and could not bear that Mae put the task off on him to do. (I think she wanted Frieda to see that he wasn't so bad. She wanted him to be a man who cared for her mother.)

I was desperate to talk to her, desperate to think she would be okay; I wanted to crawl up on her bed and lie beside her. But I couldn't appear one minute and burst in with my questions the next. I sat on a chair by her bed and put my hand on her forearm, tears dripping down my face, while she fell asleep.

The next morning I sat with her again, and I said, there are things you could tell me now. We both knew it was now or never. She patted my hand and said, I'm so tired, sugar.

Please, I said. I want to know about my father.

I felt her tighten. What would be the use in that? she said. And anyway, Edith never said.

I didn't believe her. I had never asked her because I felt she didn't want me to and because I never thought I cared, or maybe because it might be better that I didn't know. I thought maybe my mother had been raped; certainly he (mystery man; no-name father) must not have loved her. Why should I want to know his name?

Well, now I did want to know.

The secret that I wasn't Daddy's child had split open when my mother died, but I hadn't asked, *who, then?* Not when Daddy's girlfriend told me, you aren't his. Nor in 1964 when Frieda gave me my original birth certificate and told me that the father listed on it was a friend of my mother's—not my father—but a nice boy who consented to be named. I had never discussed the matter with anyone; only after Frieda died—ten years after—would Mae tell me the truth, as if it had just occurred to her that she didn't have to keep it secret anymore.

That afternoon in Lubbock, my sister arrived from Connecticut like a force of nature, and she was in the bedroom with Frieda for hours. I could hear her low voice going on and on. Once I was sure I heard Frieda crying. I opened the door and when she saw me, she shook her head. No. My aunt and I huddled, too cowed to challenge my formidable sister.

My sister left, and Frieda turned her face to the wall. In the evening, she got up and sat at the kitchen table for a while. We talked, though not about my question. I had a little time with her and in the morning, a goodbye embrace. I left with the sick awful feeling that I had lost something important in those two days and that I was about to lose my grandmother, too. I had always felt that I was inside a kind of secret circle with my grandmother, an invisible King's X, a place that other people didn't see. Now I realized that my sister knew I felt I had a special right to our grandmother, and she had come to shatter it. It's all speculation; maybe I am unfair to my sister, overly suspicious, or maybe I am right, and we—Frieda and I—had it coming. My sister would certainly never discuss it with me, and I never saw my grandmother again. It's not right, though, to have someone wrested from you just before you are going to lose her.

In July I told Frieda I would come to Wichita Falls with my daughter. I would be with her as long as she wanted.

She said she didn't want company.

She kept secrets—not, I think, to hide anything shameful, but because she wasn't a storyteller and she didn't see the point of talking about things long gone. Maybe she thought of her story as private—if she thought of her life as story at all. Maybe she didn't see the point of raking wounds. (I feel sure that the idea of talk therapy would baffle her, as would books by rich widows grieving the deaths of old husbands, or this book, for that matter.) I didn't know until a few years ago that she had married in Arizona in 1940 so that she could move to Gallup, New Mexico, and bring her children to live with her after years apart. The husband, Joe, had been her husband Ira's friend in Chickasha, Oklahoma; I imagine that he wanted to look after her not only for his friend's sake but also for his own and Frieda's, for though she was stalk thin and bone tired, she was still a young and pretty woman. Perhaps he had been shocked when he found her cooking for a railroad section gang in Apache, making three hundred dollars a year in hard circumstances. The whole matter came up when I came across Frieda's social security card with his last name on it. (Oh him! Mac said. Good heavens.) It was hard to make sense of her cool pragmatism, though I tried in my last novel, *Plain Seeing*, in which family stories inspired much of the plot. I had the grandmother (called Greta) marry a railroad man, ". . . famous for his daring. He loved to walk the tops of the cars, especially at night, when they had to count on strings stretched across the tracks to warn workers before they came into a tunnel . . . Greta enjoyed his pride, his high spirits."

I hope Frieda's marriage gave her some pleasure, an easing of her loneliness. Maybe she didn't want a partner; she wanted her children. The war took him away; separating was in someone else's hands.

* * *

Joe wrote Edith on April 19, 1943, while he was away in the service. Edith had written him to tell him that she was pregnant. By then Frieda and the children were in Wichita Falls.

He wrote back to urge her to "keep your chin up." He wrote:

> . . . I sure would like to see you all move to Chickasha but I am leaving it up to your mother from now on. I am not ever going to suggest any thing [sic] any more [sic] because if any thing [sic] turns up I get the blame and I am through taking blame. I have tried to do my best to make her happy but I have given up and all I can do now is send the allotments and hope to God things turn out the best.

If "the best" was another chance to make a family with Frieda and her children, it didn't happen. He never saw them again.

I think she thought that when something passed there was no reason for it to be discussed, because what could talking do that time hadn't? She was a fatalist. I am sure now that she was deeply in love with her husband, the father of her children, Ira; that, despite their economic plight, she was happy for a time. He died young, and from that everything flowed: hardship, anger, loneliness, forgetting. She learned a terrible lesson early, and the worst of it was that she could not save her children from her grief.

WHAT WE LOST TO GRIEF

We lost men.

Those who died, of course: Frieda's father, Wilhelm. Her husband Ira. Someone I loved, dying young. Baby boys. But I am thinking of the men we couldn't love or who didn't love us. The men who didn't stay, the ones who couldn't be found. You heard the door slam but you didn't know where he had gone. Men were extraneous. They kept proving themselves to be just what she expected. We couldn't depend on them. We sent them packing, if they didn't take off first. She did, Mother did, my aunt did, I did, my cousins did.

Didn't I tell you? She didn't say it, but it must have hung in the air.

She would have done anything for her son, of course, but the pain he caused her never went away. How could it? He had been the sweetest boy, the dearest son, and then too much went wrong. He boiled with blame and resentment. His anger—at bosses, at the Army, at banks and businesses, at bridges and buildings, at her and at his wife, his sister, his sons—was her anger, too; the way his blood was hers. In Korea, he was the only soldier in his tank to survive; he came home deaf in one ear, a punished man. If he borrowed money—and he did—she cosigned, and he hated owing her. The last time she left her house, it was to pay off his debt. It was like saying, I know you'll never do it. There was no way to give it back. The only thing he could do was make trouble for the rest of us.

He was a fatherless son, lost and never found.

We lost my mother, and with her the fragile alliance that was a family. There went her husband, Dean—Karen's daddy and, so I had believed, mine; what did you expect?

He would have said: Without Edith, I don't have a stamp to stand on.

He wasn't going to get in a fight over kids. He had a different life in mind. He was thirty-one years old.

We lost trust.

The Hambletons stole Ira's insurance, and Frieda couldn't afford her own children.

Dean sold my piano and married a redheaded floozy.

The mill shut down just before the first full pensions would have been due.

Strangers had no stake in us; you had to be wary. Promises flowed away like water. Family was all you had, and then hearts could turn to stone. You could work like coolies and find yourself cast out. One day it was summer, and overnight the earth turned to ice.

Is it any wonder that she grasped anger, a sure thing she could hold?

We lost each other some of the time. All the things we couldn't say, wouldn't say, dared not say, like moats between us. Slam a door, squeal a wheel, hang up a phone. Then let it go—not away, not every time, but out of sight. No matter what, there was next time. Whatever it was my sister said to Frieda in Lubbock, I would have made things better if I had gone to my grandmother when she went home to Wichita Falls. I will forever regret that I did not. If my grandmother hadn't wanted to talk, she wouldn't have had to. I wouldn't have bothered her with questions. I might not have talked at all.

THE LAST FARMER

F rieda's mother, Mathilde, was a Volberding. There were—are—so many of them. Almost thirty years ago a distant relative—a second-cousin-twice-removed—contacted various members of my family, and eventually me, to say that he was trying to organize a family history. The information that he sent me, along with the information now available online, gives me a line of German heritage that goes back as far as the birth of Johann Friedrich Volberding in Rodewald on February 8, 1746. My cousin worked with genealogists in Germany and ultimately made a trip there to visit the farm where Johann Friedrich had lived and where in the nearby Lutheran Church he had had the duties of a "Kirchen-Jurator," or elder, whose primary role was to pass a pouch on a stick to collect contributions.

Friedrich's son, Johann Jurgen, was Mathilde's grandfather. He was one of fourteen children. He and his first wife had nine children. After he was widowed, he married again. Their first son Wilhelm was born in Germany, and there were three more sons born after they too emigrated. Immigration occurred in 1850—the beginning of a decade in which almost a million Germans would come to America. Family lore has it that Mathilde's father, Friedrich August, was born on the ship, but as far as I know, no one was able to substantiate that.

Rodewald is now a village of two thousand inhabitants, located in Lower Saxony between Hanover and Bremen. It was in the Middle Ages a duchy handed down son to son, but the family became extinct in 1582. In 1866—after the Volberdings were gone—the area was annexed by Prussia.

Farmers had been unhappy with their lot for a very long time. They were subject to military conscription; they paid onerous head-taxes; their religious freedom was curtailed. When William Penn visited the area in the seventeenth century, promising tolerance and prosperity in the New World, many families threw in with him and his American colony. Later immigrants populated the Midwest. Into the late nineteenth century, more immigrants to America were German than any other nationality. In the 1850s, refugees from the failed 1848 revolutionary efforts across Europe flooded to join settlers in America, setting up what historians call "chain migration." In short, if you were from Rodewald, you went where someone from Rodewald had gone before you.

The Volberdings were prosperous farmers, but they must have intuited that the smoldering political upheavals would threaten their holdings. Besides, there were so many of them in the family, and only so much land to go around, and America beckoned. The first Volberdings to emigrate were two sons of Johann Jurgen. Along with a few Rodewald friends, they took up 120-acre plots in an area called Franzosenbusch in Illinois. Eventually they joined with seven other families to establish a school district and build a church. Their settlement became what is now Proviso, Illinois, where many Volberdings have lived and died, including those brothers' parents and several siblings.

Five more Volberdings, including Friedrich August, went to Iowa to farm in Grant Township, Grundy County, Iowa. Eventually, August moved on to Minnesota, where Mathilde was born in 1882. Her mother was the child of immigrants from Rodewald, too. Mathilde (called Tillie) had three siblings. The oldest, Edward, fathered a large family and remained in Iowa, but Mathilde, her sister Sophie and her brother Albert, her parents, her husband, and their first child, a son, Louis, all moved to Indian territory (Oklahoma) in 1902 or 1903. There, Leonard was born in 1904, and Frieda was born in January 1906. Most members of the family were eventually buried in Devol, Oklahoma, where Mathilde and her second husband, Ulysses Sampson Hill, farmed.

It is well established: Frieda came out of Rodewald on her mother's side. Wilhelm Harms, her father, was born in Germany in 1873, and I think it is likely that he, too, came from Lower Saxony and followed the news of America to Minnesota. He emigrated as a boy of twelve along with his older sister Johanna and her fiancé, Heinrich Mohr. They sailed on the "Bohemia" from Hamburg. The 1900 census listed the three as residents of New York City, but the next year Wilhelm, only eighteen, married Mathilde in Minnesota.

I don't know how the Volberdings and Harms families made their trek to Indian Territory. It was early enough that many migrants still journeyed by wagon. But the families farmed in Alva, where Frieda was born, and so I think they arrived by train. Alva was the last stop on the railroad from Kiowa, Kansas.

Mathilde had a second daughter, Frances, with her second husband. Frieda was always close to her cousin, Velma, the daughter of Sophie. Velma was the last of the cousins to die.

When Frieda was five years old, in 1911, Wilhelm died in a farming accident. Mathilde and her children lived with her parents until 1916, when she married Ulysses Sampson Hill ("Daddy Hill"), a farmer originally from Tennessee, and moved with him to Devol, in Cotton County, where the growing season was seven months long. The little town had a population of 400. Within three years, the oil boom just across the Red River swelled the Devol population to over 4,000. (The 2010 census reported a population of 151.) Although the Hills would see boom and bust, drought and rain, in the years that followed, their manner of working and living changed little. They bought and moved a house from Devol with wagons. It was fitted for a bathroom, but they never had running water or a septic tank. They hauled in water in tanks that they parked in the dusty yard. They used chamber pots and an outhouse. They never replaced the first furniture they bought. They drove a car twenty years or more. They dressed nicely and went to church on Sundays. They had their main meal midday and leftovers or pie or milk and bread at the end of the day's work. In winter, they had a portable gas stove in the kitchen; in summer, they had fans. They wore their clothes—coveralls for Daddy, "wash dresses" for Tillie—until they were rags. They had a radio and a player piano.

Despite the immense challenge of dry land wheat farming, Mathilde and Daddy Hill survived the hardships of two wars and the Great Depression and lived into their eighties.

The history of the town of Bradley, Oklahoma, is a web of Indian history—who was moved onto the land, who was moved off of it; allotments and seizures; and eventually, ranches and farms. When Ira and Frieda Hambleton went there to farm in 1925, it is unlikely that they had any notion of the abundance the land had provided early Native Americans. The Washita River had been home to ducks, catfish, gar, and bass; the land had been home to deer, turkey, bison, and small game. An archeological excavation in the 1980s revealed that there had been fertile terraces where the people grew corn, beans, squash, and other crops.

Frieda had moved to Chickasha after her high school graduation in June 1924 in Devol, where she had been a good student and had played basketball. She had been awarded a scholarship for a secretarial course; she had every intention of escaping farm life. But she soon met Ira—I don't know how, only that it was in Chickasha. They married, and in July 1925, their first daughter, Edith Aileen, was born. Ira had no education and no special skills, but he wasn't afraid of hard work. The couple took on tenancy of a small farm and moved into its dilapidated house and struggled against drought with inadequate equipment and no help. The huge black clouds of dirt that would be heralded as the beginning of the Dust Bowl were still a few years away, but to understand what Ira's and Frieda's farm life was like, you can certainly turn to the literature and photography of the Great Depression. The photographs I have tell a clear enough story. They had a mule and a plow and a harness. They had no electricity. They hauled water in a wagon. They were hardly settled before Frieda was pregnant again; Eula Mae was born on the farm in October 1926. Their house, poorly supported on the dry soil, listed badly to the right as you looked toward their front door. The outhouse, off to the left and behind the house, leaned so far in one direction that you could have crawled under it on one side. In a picture of Frieda standing in front of the house, holding the baby Mae, with Edith in a sunbonnet beside her, the yard looks blasted or burned, utterly arid with patches of inch-high weeds. A limp three-wire fence stretches across the front of Frieda and her girls.

I have half a dozen photographs and the ostensible memories of my aunt to inform me about that period in Frieda's life. One picture, the one with the leaning house, sits on a table in my bedroom. You can see that a windowpane has been broken, but its shards not removed; someone has shoved a pillow into the open space.

I cannot describe Frieda's expression. She is neither happy nor un-happy. She is wearing a checkered dress with a pleated skirt. Her hair is bobbed. The photographs could have been taken by her younger sister, Frances, or by her older brother, Lou, both of whom had cameras. Frieda, standing there, seems to say: Here we are.

When they gave up—they had no crop, no money, no food—they went to Devol to Daddy Hill's farm.

Let's say for a moment that the farmhouse, with its three bedrooms, din-ing room, parlor, and kitchen, is Frieda's, and one of her daughters has appeared at the door with *her* children. (The husband is irrelevant.) There would be a flurry of rearranging furniture, the high energy of the kids, a bustle in the kitchen. Everyone would have a place to sleep—some perhaps on pallets of quilts on the floor—and when she woke in the morning to make breakfast, she wouldn't worry about her daughter and her children, because they are under her roof.

It must have been something like that for Tillie and her children when their Papa was killed in a farm accident in 1911. Tillie's parents housed the young family for years, until Tillie married again. Frieda spoke to me numerous times of her gentle grandparents, of how hard it was to move away from them.

But it wasn't like that for Frieda's family. Maybe Ira had proved to be what Daddy Hill and Tillie expected of a town boy. Maybe they were disappointed in Frieda. Or maybe Tillie had simply done what her husband said; he must have thought that a man had to have his own household. Besides, Frieda wasn't his daughter, and she would never forget it.

They put Frieda and Ira and their children in an old settler's cabin on the far side of the henhouse. It is difficult to imagine that Tillie felt good doing it. Dirt floor, oil lamps, extremes of heat and cold. The girls were just toddlers, so you suppose they played in the big house on cold days. Maybe Frieda and her children could have been inside while Ira hired out as a farm hand and paid Daddy Hill five dollars a month. The 1930 census lists them as "renters." Later that year they went back to Chickasha so that Frieda could have their baby in a hospital. I assume that they stayed with the Hambletons and that it was hard for Frieda, who never felt welcome in their home. Maybe it helped that the child was a boy.

Later, when a railroad job came up for Ira, and Frieda returned to the farm without him, she must have heard her mother criticize him. For what? His heroic efforts in a crumbled farm economy? His itinerant labor in the Southwest, where he constantly had trouble finding a place to live that he could afford? Frieda had three small children to care for, but she would have thrown herself into whatever work needed doing in the house or the fields. At least they lived in the house.

I didn't know anything about that time until I read Ira's letters to Frieda from Arizona. He sent money orders to her while she stayed with her folks. Ira writes, comforting her because she is unhappy, reminding her how much he loves her and the children, and that no matter what their families think of them, they will someday be together and happy again. His letters are the assurances of someone in exile to his marooned lover. He, too, felt the derision. Though Frieda's brother Lou, who had a good job with the Santa Fe Railroad, welcomed him into his home, his wife did not, and there were quarrels about a dollar here or a dollar there for food, a bed, gasoline. Ira was working as hard as he could, and he felt like a beggar. He sent money home and worried that it might be intercepted, asking in every letter: did you receive my money order? He wrote everyone he knew in Oklahoma, begging for work. In 1935 he finally sent money for Frieda to bring the children to join him, but soon after they arrived, he hurt his back, and they all returned to Chickasha. It seemed like a miracle when he got a job with the Oklahoma State Highway Department. With the little packet of savings that he and Frieda had accumulated from his railroad earnings, plus the credit of good employment, they bought a small house on a treelined street near a girls' college. It was humble, but it was *theirs*. The family was together.

CHICKASHA DAILY
CHICKASHA, OKLAHOMA, MONDAY, SEPTEMBER 28, 1936
FALL IS FATAL TO LOCAL MAN
Ira A. Hambleton Succumbs of [sic] Injuries

Funeral services for Ira A. Hambleton, age 32, were to be conducted at 3 o'clock this afternoon from the Brown Funeral Home by Rev. Monroe Wright, pastor of the Frisco Avenue Methodist Church. Burial was in the Rose Hill Cemetery.

Mr. Hambleton died late Saturday night in a local hospital from a fractured skull received when a wind caught under the tarpaulin covering supplies on the back of a state highway truck on which he was riding, throwing him to the pavement. The accident occurred late Saturday afternoon several miles from Chickasha on highway 62.

Mr. Hambleton, who was an employee of the State Highway Department, was sitting under the tarpaulin used as protection from the rain, with W. L. Jones, who though bruised was not thrown from the truck. At the time of the accident Tom Fletcher was driving the truck, and riding with him in the cab was C. F. Burkhalter.

Born in Temple, Ok., Mr. Hambleton had been a resident of Chickasha and Grady County for the past ten years. He recently had been employed with the highway department. Mr. Habmleton [sic] was a member of the Frisco Avenue Methodist Church.

Surviving members of the family include his widow, three children, Edith Alliene [sic] and Eula May [sic], a son, Louis Edward; parents, Mr. and Mrs. W. H. Hambleton; five sisters, Elza, Lona and Florene Hambleton and Mrs. Harry Weaver, all of Chickasha, and Mrs. J. W. Hamilton of Cement, and grandfather, F. A. Hambleton of Chickasha.

I can only assume that Ira's father was the informant for the reporter who wrote this front page article, since Ira's widow, Frieda, was not even named, though all the men on the truck with her husband were and all the Hambleton kin were; furthermore, both of their daughters' names were misspelled.

Ira's father signed the death certificate.

Ira's supervisor sent Frieda and the children a ham.

Ira had a substantial life insurance policy through the state, but he had let his father use it as collateral to borrow money. When Ira died, his father considered the debt forgiven. Despite the plight of his son's family, he refused to repay the debt or to offer any assistance to Frieda so that she could keep her house or, for that matter, so that she could keep her children with her.

It isn't hard to understand her deep and lasting anger toward Ira's father ever after and her resentment that Edith maintained Hambleton bonds. It isn't hard to understand that she would never depend on anyone for anything.

Frieda never saw any of the Hambletons again. Some time later, the children were sent by Frieda's mother from the Devol farm to Chickasha to visit them, but when Sonny was upbraided for asking if he could use some toothpaste, he swore he would never step foot in their house again, and he didn't. (He so loved Frieda's mother, on the other hand, that he asked to be buried by her.)

Only Edith maintained a relationship with the Hambletons, primarily because she was so fond of Ira's sweet sister Elza, a morbidly obese woman who never left her parents' home and who made a modest living as a seamstress.

* * *

You couldn't say that Frieda didn't try. She found a job as a file clerk in the county clerk's office. She moved all three children into her bedroom and rented the second bedroom to a couple of college girls. She wrote the admission office at the secretarial college where she had been awarded a scholarship at her high school graduation. The school was right there in Chickasha. She had begun a program there but halfway through the year had dropped out to marry Ira. Now she thought that if she could complete the program and earn its certificate, she could get a better paying office job. Maybe she thought she could take classes while working, as long as she didn't have to come up with the money for tuition. Or maybe a stipend had been included in the scholarship.

An administrator wrote back that a fire had destroyed their files; they had no record of her award or of her attendance. She was invited to come to the school and discuss her situation so that they could see what they could do. The letter was apologetic and courteous. Frieda did not go to see them, did not go to school, did not find a better job, but for some reason saved the letter—one more artifact of her bad luck and cast-off ambitions.

Edith and Mae, eleven and ten years old, learned from the boarders that a lot of food was thrown away at the end of the day in the college cafeteria. They went to the school and talked to someone who said that if the girls would help sweep and wash up, they could take some of the leftovers home. Mae remembers ham bones and wilted salads, but after a short while, a supervisor put a stop to the barter. Charity, she said, was not her mission. Next the girls went around the neighborhood offering their services as babysitters, but no one thought they were old enough.

The boarders went home for the summer. Frieda advertised for someone new, but no one suitable appeared. Her five-dollar-a-week job wasn't enough to pay the sixteen dollar monthly mortgage, utilities, and food. There was nothing she could do but go to her mother and stepfather, though she must have thought about how they had treated Ira. Tillie brought it up. She knew what it was like to lose your young husband when you had three children and nothing of your own. She had cleaned houses for years, until she married again. She understood that Frieda would get nothing from her snotty English in-laws. Enough was enough. There were the children to consider.

You had better come to the farm, she wrote. We'll figure something out.

I grew up hearing many stories about myself: the tantrums, the precocity, the time I crawled under the house and fell asleep and everyone went looking for me in backyards up and down the street. Not so many stories got told about others in the family, but all of them were comic or tender— except for the one about Frieda leaving her children at the farm in Devol and going away for four years like a sailor gone to sea. I think I first heard about it from my cousin Glenda, the daughter of Frieda's sister. I thought it sounded made-up. Now I remember that she also told me I was adopted, which wasn't quite the right story, and I certainly didn't believe her.

My grandfather, killed by a dust devil. My grandmother, leaving her children on the farm. I don't think I believed these things actually happened until I was an adult, but, *as a story*, it was compelling, a distant tale, like wagon train journeys. How was it possible to be so desperate? Sometimes at the farm I crawled under my great-grandmother's bed in the room by the kitchen, and I pretended I was hearing the ghosts of children crying. There was a story about orphaned babies that I told myself, because it was so sad and I loved sad stories, but I didn't believe it was true. And when, eventually, I did suspect that the story had come from my family's history and not from my imagination, I put it out of my mind, because I could not bear to imagine my mother's tears, or her mother's tears, or—and wasn't this the heart of it?—my own. I'll never have children, I told myself. I thought I could save them, and myself, all heartache. They just would not be.

* * *

You raise children so that they will have their own lives, and then you are supposed to go on having your life without them. They are not supposed to lose a parent while they are young and needy, and if they do, maybe you feel compelled to make up for their loss for the rest of your life. It isn't hard for me, now that I have a grown daughter of my own, to understand why Frieda could never abandon her children to their fates, whatever their culpability, whatever their age. Because isn't family the only real safety net?

I have probed that question in my stories. In my novel *Beyond Deserving*, a woman feels she has to choose between her husband and her daughter, and she gives the child to her mother to raise. In *Opal on Dry Ground*, two grown daughters move in with their mother when their lives fall apart. In *More Than Allies*, a young mother whose husband has left her lives with her foster mother. I didn't set out to prove a thesis about a mother's love, but I do wonder how anyone ever knows when—if—it's wrong to help your kids.

Of course a novel doesn't have just one thematic string. A friend pointed out to me once that in my fiction, there's always someone looking for a place to live. Houses are like slippery characters that never quite settle down.

I didn't grow up until I had a child. I had had jobs and travels, lovers, and a husband, but I had never understood how serious life is until I had the responsibility for someone else's. I didn't know what I was doing—I had no family nearby, and Dr. Spock was the only expert in print—but I wanted to be a good mother. I tried to arrange my life to make that possible. I put my daughter first. In many ways, I always have. But you could also say she gave me the greater gift by cleansing me of my selfishness.

And if she needed me a little more, or a little longer, than other children need their mothers, that was okay with me. And when her college years and young adulthood were interrupted by spasms of illness and doubt, I was on call. Back and forth she went; back and forth I went. The one thing I knew was that I had to be there, because if I wasn't, who would be?

When my husband and I moved to Montana in 2005, after thirty years in Oregon, I was terribly lonely. My daughter came from New York to be with me for a year and then decided to stay in the West to be near us. My turn, she said. And when she had her child in Oregon, I spent two years with them there, because she was a single mother, and because I was so happy to be a grandmother.

Let go. I have heard it often from well-meaning friends. I will, I say, but I don't say *soon*. One day letting go will be out of my hands, and even now I am practicing acceptance, something I don't really need to do. I don't think: *I'll be dead*. I think: *I'll be gone*. And though I am confident she will be okay when she is finally without me, *I* miss *her* already.

I t was late fall of 1937, and there was frost on the ground. Everyone was up before first light. Frieda was ready to go. She took her bag out to her brother Lou's car first thing. He had found her a job with the Santa Fe Railroad, cooking for section gangs across New Mexico and Arizona.

She brought water from the barrel on the porch into the kitchen and made breakfast for the men: Lou and their stepfather, Daddy Hill, and their mother's brother, Uncle Albert. The men ate without talk, slurping their coffee.

Albert rose and patted Frieda on the shoulder, then went to the barn. Lou accompanied Daddy Hill to the wheat field. Lou had never taken up the plow himself, but he liked to watch the day break with a farmer.

Frieda made another batch of biscuits and bacon and watched her children creep into the kitchen with their wounded faces: Edith, age twelve and frail as a stalk of cracked glass; Eula Mae, a year younger but stalwart; and Sonny, seven, looking like a miniature Ira, with high cheekbones and bright eyes.

They sat with Frieda's mother at the table, all of them quiet, hardly able to swallow. Her mother said, the children will thrive. Milk and eggs, chores and school.

Frieda added: church and waiting.

At that, Sonny sprang up and ran outside, banging doors. He was still his mother's baby, and her face went grim. Edith gave a cry and threw herself facedown in Frieda's lap. Mae didn't budge. When Frieda's mother got up to clear the table, Mae collected all the silverware and carried it to the sink. By then, Daddy Hill and Lou had come to the kitchen door.

Frieda said, Mae, you look after Sonny and mind Mama all the ways you can.

She didn't say anything to Edith, but touched her face with her fingers.

There was nothing left but leaving. Children sobbing on the steps. The awful waving. Daddy Hill stood to the side, his hands tucked into the bib of his overalls. Sonny would thrive on the farm and grow up adoring his grandma. Mae would take the blame for his infractions—who let the parakeet out! She would do chores and pray and have her hair permed with electric curlers, because her grandmother wanted her to. Edith floated through the months, through the years; when she got bored with farm life, she went to the Hambletons in Chickasha. She came home with barrettes, a new comb. A cousin taught her to drive. Mae can't remember anyone ever scolding her for anything.

It would be four years before Frieda would bring her children to Gallup, New Mexico to join her. A year after that the war would save them: Frieda took a factory job as a pony packer at General Mills in Wichita Falls, across the river from her mother's farm. She packed flour for a quarter of a century and remembered where it came from. She never wasted a mouthful of food. Everything had been grown, tended, picked, prepared, packaged. It bothered her that children didn't appreciate the labor in the things they took for granted. She sent us out to water her garden. She had us string green beans, peel potatoes, sort pinto beans. On the farm, she sat on the porch step with me beside her, plucking feathers from a chicken. *Ew,* I'd say, and she'd laugh, but it was memorable instruction.

She worked in nursing homes and cared for her aged parents in her own house. She would not turn earth again until she built a house on Grant Street in Wichita Falls in 1953. She raised okra and tomatoes and onions, year and after year, until Tillie left the farm to die in Frieda's house. Then there was no time to dig and plant and water, and by then Frieda didn't care much about food anyway.

Her mother was the last farmer in Frieda's line. She is buried, as is Frieda, with so many other Volberdings and their husbands and children, in Devol, Oklahoma.

Frieda left her children and went to work for the Santa Fe Railroad as a cook for section gangs. She lived and worked in a boxcar. She wrote her children every week. And of course she sent her mother her wages to pay for the children's upkeep. These were the years of the Great Depression. The Hills kept chickens and turkeys and a cow. They tended a kitchen garden; there was always food, but Frieda's wages were significant income in those years when crops were bad. Almost a year before she brought the other children to Gallup, she sent for Edith. The two of them couldn't bear the separation. Edith's departure for New Mexico is one of Mae's bitterest memories, but she tells it matter-of-factly. It was like that, Mother and Edith.

I saw a small photograph of Frieda once while I was living with her in Wichita Falls. It was in a drawer under the towels, probably put there long ago and forgotten. She was skinny as a stick, dressed in a simple cotton dress, standing on the ground in front of the car where she lived. I didn't know what to make of it. I asked her where it was taken, what she had been doing. She said she had worked in New Mexico and Arizona for a while. She said the crews wanted biscuits, bacon, and gravy every morning.

I reckon I've made about 50,000 biscuits, she said.

I got a better idea of what it might have been like for her when I read the 1940 census for Apache, Arizona. There were 130 households, many with lodgers. Frieda identified herself as a cook and was living with a "helper," a Mexican woman. Frieda said that she had made three hundred dollars in 1939. She said that she worked fifty hours a week and that she paid fifty cents a week rent. (Whether for a boxcar or a house I don't know, but four dollars a month appeared to be a usual rent for a house. You wonder what houses were like.) One of the questions was, where were you in 1935? Frieda said that she was in Maricopa, Arizona; Mae says they all had all gone out to join Ira, but Ira hurt his back, and they returned to Chickasha. Dozens of other people reported that they had been living "someplace."

There are a couple of salesmen (curio stones, petrified wood); salt mine laborers; cowboys. And many railroad section hands, the men who ate Frieda's meals. Some reported incomes as high as eight hundred dollars; others less.

While I was writing this, the electricity went off for an hour. The irony of my reaction didn't hit me until later.

I thought: how will I finish my work? How will I make dinner? *How will I cope?*

BELOVED

SUFFERING

When Edith, Frieda's first-born child, was three years old, she had scarlet fever. Her throat and skin burned red and she cried out deliriously. The family was living on a tenant farm in Bradley, Grady County, Oklahoma, not far from Chickasha. It was drought barren and bleak. To get out of the dust, the little girls spent whole days under a table that had been covered with a sheet. There were no antibiotics. There was no doctor. Frieda took Edith out in the yard and dribbled cups of precious water over her face and chest. Edith survived, a girl and then a woman of ethereal beauty, but Frieda worried about her for the rest of her life. Edith was never wholly well. Frieda worried and lived on call, like a soldier or a duty nurse. Like a lover, a mother. The only times that she ever missed work at the mill were when Edith was sick. It didn't matter if they hadn't spoken in months. Once Edith moved to Odessa, Frieda made a lot of trips on short notice. Edith wanted her own life, but she needed her mother most of the time.

Edith was a beautiful child. She looked like an angel, with her cotton white hair, her long tender arms and legs. She always seemed to need looking after. Lie down a while. Have a glass of tea. Here's a cool rag for your forehead. Nobody expected much of her, and knowing that she had so little strength, everyone wondered that she had ambition and that she had children. Poor Edith, you'd have heard it said of her, and you'd have known most everyone thought she was dreamy and foolish, though they loved her.

If she had been stronger, she might have made her way through school. She would have had to be an optimist—no, a visionary—to see her way out of poverty. Two months after I was born, she had someone take a snapshot of her posing bathing beauty style in a two-piece sun suit, sitting sideways on Frieda's rickety slab of a porch. She had just turned eighteen. She must have been thinking she had a future. She wanted to be an actress or an artist; she wanted to be a teacher or a writer; she wanted to be in the thick of politics. She wanted to have her own home, dishes, silverware; she wanted her children to study music and art and swimming; she wanted to travel. I think she converted to Catholicism because it was intellectually and aesthetically rich, and because it opened gates to education for my sister and me. And of course it helped explain her suffering in a way that comforted her.

Frieda wondered where Edith got all her high-minded ideas.

When she should have been a freshman in high school, she was at her Hambleton grandparents' home in Chickasha, resting and reading until her mother sent for her to come to Gallup. In New Mexico, she lied about her age and worked as a Harvey Girl at the grand depot restaurant. After a month the railroad sent her to Winslow, Arizona, to work and board. Her boyfriend, Jack, could see that waitressing was too much for her and that she was lonely; he took her back to her home, a railroad car on a dusty lot in Gallup. She must have been waiting all the time for things to get better, for something to happen. For love, opportunity, luck. She had been born into hardship, but she was always favored with what there was. If there was one orange, Edith ate it.

Edith, seventeen, was pregnant when Frieda moved her children from Gallup, New Mexico, to Wichita Falls, Texas, the week before Christmas 1942. Factories were looking for women to fill the jobs men had left to go to war, and Frieda knew she could better her life in a union shop.

Edith didn't know she was pregnant, so her mother didn't know; her boyfriend, Jack, didn't know. Jack tells me they had had a great romance. When she was a Harvey Girl living in a dormitory, he would drive to Winslow to spend an hour with her sitting in the car after her shift. In Gallup he wanted to be with her whenever he wasn't working. She was full of dreams and fancy words. She was so beautiful. He told her life was going to get good. He was a go-getter; he had the dashing looks of a rake. His family was fatherless, too, like hers, but he knew he could work hard and make deals and do all right. At nineteen, he was running a gas station. He had a Model A.

They wrote letters to each other and dotted them with their blood and buried them in a metal box on a bluff. One afternoon in November they went there, to their special place, and they were caught in a snowstorm. He had blankets. There was just that one time.

Jack tells me he went to Dallas in December to buy used tires for the station, and the Hambletons were gone when he got back. It socked the breath out of him, the sight of that empty lot where they had been living in a railroad car. Soon after, he went to San Diego and joined the Navy. Just before he shipped out a few months later, Edith appeared, pregnant and sick. She thought she was going to lose the baby. She had taken a bus from Wichita Falls to look for him. Jack, at ninety, though supremely sentimental about my mother and about me, can't remember if Edith wrote him, if he wrote her, if there was a misunderstanding. Her appearance was a total surprise.

In fact, I have several letters from him to Edith. (I can only wonder if Frieda ever looked at them; my guess is she didn't. Why would she want to know what he had to say? But then, why would she save them? They probably went with other things of my mother's into a box on North Lamar, got moved to Frieda's next house on Grant Street, and stored, all without any further examination. The cache of letters in that box is a random collection, and it's just luck that the odd lot holds so much history.) In one letter he says that they might "work something out when this [*the war*] is over," but by then Edith had married someone else. He wrote her in Wichita Falls. He wrote her in Indiana. In his letters he sounds practical and wary. He made a trip to Chicago in 1946—to propose to a woman (her family had moved there from Gallup) who turned him down—and made a side trip to check on Edith. She was married with a new baby, and me. He had a lot going on.

Jack saw their possibilities for the pie-in-the-sky they were by then, and he was eager to go home to New Mexico and start constructing a life. He has worked out an uncomplicated, if mysterious, explanation for their ill-fated romance; the real mystery is what Edith was thinking. She never saw or heard from him again. I'm sure that she felt trapped and desperate, and her husband, Dean, probably did too. They didn't fight, but they had nothing in common except their child. I think she had hoped that, pretty and precocious as I was, Jack wouldn't be able to go away without me—which meant her, too—but he wasn't occupying the same version of the universe that she was. Hard as it is for me to say, Jack wasn't impressed. He went on to marry and have six children. That day in Indiana he saw me as a cute kid attached to another man's life, naught to do with him. Edith didn't know him so very well: he wanted a forthright, uncomplicated life, with a family and his own business. (Who wouldn't?) He wouldn't have wanted to get caught up in Edith's unhappiness. She had made her bed by then. The same attributes that made him a consummate businessman made him a vanished prospect.

In my heart of hearts I ache for my mother. If there was any romance in their last encounter, it was in her expectations, and most certainly not in Jack's, but I can accept his memories for what they are—romantic fragments and tales. He's near the end of his life, and he's engaged in constructing its narrative; that is an understandable, even admirable, enterprise. He sees his memories of my mother as a gift to me. The myth of my beginning. I accept it. I am trying to construct my own understanding of the past, and it doesn't require that it match up with his or that I set him straight. He is my father, yes, but he was never family.

The past is an illusion, and I expect that the closer we come to the end of our lives, the more we choose some parts and let all the rest slide away. I am anguished when I try to imagine my mother's regrets at the end of her life. Thirty-three, marooned in West Texas on a pile of lost dreams. I've written about her, and now I'm trying to choose memories to hold on to and let the saddest parts fade.

So there's another story about Jack. It hadn't taken long for him to give up on Edith. (He figured her mother put her foot down when they moved; she was just seventeen and headstrong. He knew Frieda thought that he was too old for her and maybe no good. And besides, he had no idea where they had gone.) He went to California and with the bright snap of a page too quickly turned, married a girl who had followed him from Gallup. Lots of young people did that; you didn't know who would come back and who wouldn't. When Edith showed up, afraid of losing the baby, with no one else to turn to, there wasn't much he could do, but he put her in the hospital. He paid the bill. He put her on a train home. Then he tried to explain himself to his young wife, who wouldn't listen. While he was in the Pacific, she divorced him, but by then he was in the Philippines. He couldn't have done anything to make things right with Edith, even if he had had time to think about it.

When he told me his story fifty years later, he still had the hospital invoice—all he had left of her.

Edith's illnesses were sometimes sudden—a rush to the hospital in the middle of the night—and sometimes insidious and long running. She had jaundice, hepatitis, ulcers, a hemorrhage, and a hysterectomy. She had migraine and nausea, edema, and intractable pain. And there were her attacks of despair, her moaning, desperate, wrist-cutting depression. Sometimes Edith was too ill to make the necessary decisions about her care, and then she resented what had been done and who had decided for her. The worst time was when Edith's doctors and her confessor thought the situation was dire: blood on the sheets, Edith's face white as wax. Her husband couldn't say what to do; he knew there was no way he would have the right answer. Frieda took her to Dallas to a state-supported sanitarium. She was there for months. She came home cowed and stony silent, with little red leather bags she had stitched in art therapy. (Here, she said to me when she gave me one of the pouches. Put something in it.) Her hair had changed; it was limp and thin, the color dull. It had been the Middle Ages at the sanitarium: cold baths, shock treatments, a terrible loneliness in the midst of bedlam. The only drugs had been ones that made her helpless. She told her mother she would never forgive her, though I think she did; it's more likely that Frieda never forgave herself. After a while, life picked up again. My sister and I hadn't really missed her, but we were very glad she was back. And Dean, lying in the dark in the back bedroom of his mother-in-law's house? He must have whispered to her, his hot hands holding her arm: I'll get us out of here, I promise, Edith. I'll get us our own place. How could he have known that before he made something of himself, Edith would be dead?

He managed to get a laborer's job in construction, and we moved into a welfare complex of cinder block duplexes. In another year, we rented a house in a nicer neighborhood on a bluff above the football stadium. We almost never saw my grandmother; I talked to her on the phone on Sundays. Then Dean got work in the oilfields and moved us to Odessa. The Sisters at my school, members of the religious order Sisters of St. Mary of Namur, were aghast at the idea that I would leave them for a town with no Catholic school. For a nominal tuition, they were giving me what amounted to a gifted education, including piano lessons, French, and time out of regular class for advanced reading and art projects. I had recently won a diocesan writing contest and a statewide piano competition for my age group. They didn't care that my parents had no money; they could send what money they could when they could. I boarded with the Sisters in Wichita Falls for two years and then I spent two more years in Fort Worth, where the religious order's high school had more to offer, including debate and drama. I don't know what my mother paid them, but it couldn't have been very much. When I went to Fort Worth, my grandmother sent me packages of fudge and cookies, women's magazines, and new panties. Once I took the bus to see her. She thought the Sisters were kind, but I could have lived with her.

I have a letter Edith wrote to Frieda in the late fall of 1958.

> Please come as soon as you can. Can you bring me a TV? It's
> so lonely and boring, I'm in bed all the time. Please come,
> Mother, I need you.

Frieda took an extended leave from General Mills. She slept in a small corner room off the kitchen. At the same time, I got sick of boarding school. I had migraines all the time, and I was so thin the mistress of boarders made me eat snacks at midmorning, after school, and before bed, and she gave me B12 shots once a week. I wanted my mother. I went home on the bus. Everything I owned fit in a small suitcase. I left my blue wool uniforms to be passed on to someone poor.

I corresponded with my speech teacher from the Fort Worth school until her death. I used the money from my first story prize to go visit her and the other old nuns who still lived in the five story brick building. I typed her autobiography for her, near the end of her life. Once I borrowed a thousand dollars from the order. I called them when my mother died, when my baby died, when my baby's father died, when my grandmother died. I didn't really think their prayers would do any good, but it comforted me to know they cared about me. I will forever be grateful to them for their generosity, even if I laugh now at some of the restrictions and requirements we girls endured. Nine years with the Sisters of St. Mary of Namur were the core of my education, not just in grammar and analysis and speaking and academic discipline but in charity and forgiveness. But I wish I had been with my mother. I envy my sister, who was with her when I was not, and I am filled with sorrow that she does not remember our mother with love and gratitude. I wish our mother had felt unable to be apart from me.

* * *

I was terrified by the huge high school in Odessa, but there were programs in debate and drama with excellent teachers and friendly participants, so I got through my classes by looking forward to the extracurricular activities. I came home in the late afternoons and stayed in my mother's room for hours, doing homework or reading in the chair at the foot of her bed. Sometimes we talked, but a lot of the time she slept or lay on her side staring toward the window. I remember that there were filmy white curtains that became gray over the winter. My aunt drove over from Kermit with her kids almost every weekend. There was an air of anticipation; we all wanted to be together. I had a boyfriend, my first, a really nice boy who was my partner in chemistry lab, and sometimes the two of us sat on Edith's bed and joked with her instead of going out. Sometimes in the middle of the night, I crawled in bed with Frieda. Then school began to feel too noisy, frantic, foreign. My migraines were worse than ever. Little by little I grew grim and sullen. I quarreled with my boyfriend over Sandra Dee. I let chemistry slide, and the teacher had a talk with me.

Edith drifted away in a fog of pain and leaden lethargy. I thought it was taking forever. Her death seemed inevitable—and unthinkable. It went back to her childhood fever; eventually doctors had diagnosed abscesses that the fever—surely a strep infection—had caused on her kidneys, the kind of diagnosis that comes late and useless. Her whole life, she had been fragile. You could look back and see how she had bloomed for such a little while, then started her long decline. On her death certificate, the doctor wrote for "duration of illness"—the nephritis, or Bright's Disease, as it was called then—*fourteen years*. It had always been there, but worsened after my birth. Off and on, up and down, that was my mother's life, and thus my grandmother's, too.

All of us were there in the room when she died: her mother, her children, her sister and brother, her beloved doctor, her husband. A priest came and went. Frieda fainted; she was mute and clumsy, something broken, for weeks. Then she rallied. There was nothing more to do for Edith, but there was me.

They didn't kill her; her death wasn't their fault. Unless the doctor helped her exit. Frieda always thought he had, that maybe he couldn't bear that she suffered so. Or maybe he was tired of watching her die. Maybe he was all give-out; he was her main support emotionally and financially as well as medically. Dean had moved into a rented room a few blocks away. He was around; I never heard them quarreling, but Edith didn't want him staying in the house. She waited all day for Dr. Tommy to come after his rounds. He sat in a chair by her bed for an hour or more every night. He brought her magazines from his office. Often she was too tired to talk. Frieda had her own routine with him. She made him a cup of coffee or tea; sometimes he had a sandwich or a piece of pie. Often he stood on the front porch talking with her. It frustrated her that she didn't fully understand what was happening to her daughter. She thought Edith should be in a hospital; Tommy said she wanted to be home. He could keep her more comfortable in her own bed, and less frightened. Wherever she was, she wasn't going to get well. I think right then Frieda decided that she would study nursing. And when she did, the year after Edith's death, she couldn't help going over those last days again and again. Edith's pallor. Her pulse. The way her eyes looked at the end. A few years before Frieda died, she told me Tommy had given Edith a shot the night before she died, and then he had gone in the bathroom and sobbed. She sounded accusatory. She couldn't see what Edith was to him, or he to her; she couldn't accept that he was in pain, like the rest of us.

I resented Tommy's visits, the closed door, but when I grew up enough to see things from Edith's point of view, I was grateful for those years of his kindly, intelligent, weary company. She felt better when he was there. She had a little happiness. They were in love, whatever that meant. It was like her heady embrace of Catholicism: full of feeling and faith. She told me, he'll see to it you go to college.

I think it was the first time anyone had loved my mother for who she truly was. I'm sure she thought he was the only man she had ever known who was smart enough to understand her.

There's no untangling the strings of mystery about Edith and Jack, Frieda and the move, the trip to California. When I read Jack's letters to my mother, I hear the same pragmatism that I hear now when he drives me around Gallup and tells me stories about buying and selling. He learned when to push and when to back off. I believe him when he says he loved her madly and would have married her—if she had written him right away. But there was a war on, and things moved fast for young men. Edith had a pocket of time when she might have worked things out with him. I think she didn't want to right then. I think she was quixotic and immature and didn't really believe what was happening to her. Maybe she wanted to see if something better would come along. She still thought she would have choices. Then she started feeling the baby inside her, and she knew she had to do something fast, but it was months too late to go looking for Jack.

She came back from California with a drugstore wedding band and news that she was married. She didn't say anything about Jack. She told her mother that she had gone out to California to marry Albert, a young man her own age who had lived up the street from them in Gallup. He was crazy about her. He said sure he could love her baby like his own. But Edith looked for Jack first, and when she tried to reach Albert later, she learned he was already on a ship at sea. Letters to her from relatives—and from Albert—were addressed to Mrs. Edith B——. Frieda liked Albert. He was a nice boy. She knew he wasn't my father, but she liked him better than the flashy one with the Model A. Albert would have done. She believed Edith when she said they had married—until she went downtown to apply for benefits for Edith and me.

Albert came home on leave to make good on his promise, but the story goes that my mother wouldn't come out of her room. Aunt Mae took time off from her job to squire him around Wichita Falls, and Frieda fed him hearty home cooking, but he never got an explanation for Edith's behavior. Not long after, she wrote him to apologize and to say she was ready now; she had been afraid he couldn't love her. (None of which I believe. She was in trouble again, and he was the only way she thought she could get out of her mother's house.) She was too late; he had met a girl and bought her a ring. He hoped Edith would be happy, too. How it must have stung Edith, this new miscalculation. His letter was in the box from Frieda's house; she had to have read it, then or later. I wonder if she felt sad for Edith, who didn't do better as she moved on. I wonder if she thought, I don't think I ever knew that child. I never knew what she was thinking.

Frieda might have been surprised if she had learned what a good catch Jack would have been. He came home from the war with money from poker games on his ship and opened an auto body shop. He sent his little brother to college. He became one of the men who built Gallup into a town that served the Navajo Nation and moviemakers, tourists, and a growing local population. He had a gift for seeing where the opportunities were, what people needed, and what kind of deal he could make to get things done. If you weren't afraid of heavy machinery and long days, you could build a business. He was the iconic postwar American success story, a man who worked hard, guessed right, had some cunning. He rubbed two nickels and made a dollar. He had a soft-drink delivery franchise and a car dealership. He dealt in cars and trucks, rock and gravel, construction. Land was cheap. He brought in metal and built an industrial park. He had five sons and a daughter—only two of them went to college; the others built businesses and got rich. Jack is frugal and savvy. He is respected and admired in his church and his town. And he took me into his life with an open heart. He rescued me from the rancor and acid of the secret that had burdened me from the age of fifteen.

Of course there's little doubt that he did better without my mother. She would never have had the stamina for his life, though maybe he would have had the money to make hers last a little longer.

A word about Jack and the auto body shop. It was a shed on a hill at the edge of town. He added a couple rooms onto it and moved in to live there. When he married, he added a kitchen. As they had children, he added more bedrooms. The house, where he lives to this day, sprawls out from its core: the shop. Recently the two of us stood in the house, and he pointed toward a wall with a large window: that's where the cars came in. He turned around and faced the entry to his bedroom: and that was where we piled the parts.

I can't help thinking that Frieda would like him now. She would appreciate a man who didn't forget his beginnings, who didn't take on airs. She would be glad he has been generous to me. She would like his house.

1944. Edith wanted to marry Albert because she was pregnant again, but he was engaged to someone else by then. She could have turned to Frieda, of course, but she didn't. She decided for herself what to do; she made arrangements through a lawyer for the baby to be adopted. It was months before Frieda asked her, don't we have something we need to talk about? Edith said, no, she didn't want to talk. She just wanted time to pass.

1982. The year before Frieda's heart attack, a man from Palo Alto, California, called her to ask if she had any information about a woman who might have rented a house on North Lamar from her in March 1945. The woman, of course, was Edith, and he was asking because he was executor of his father's estate, and he had discovered his own adoption papers. His name was Jeff.

He was methodical, determined, and clever. He looked up every birth of a baby boy in Wichita Falls on his birth date. One by one, he tracked them down through announcements and records—graduations, real estate, marriages—but there was one child for whom there were no records after his birth. He was able to see the original hospital record, with his mother's name on it. Edith Hambleton. He looked up the address she had given the hospital. It had been owned by Frieda Hambleton, so he figured he had found his way in. It was so easy. Frieda was listed in the phone book, living at a different address now. He called and said, softly, courteously, that he was doing some genealogical research and she might be able to help him. That was all he needed to say.

You're her son, Frieda said. She invited him to come and see her. He flew to Texas and spent most of a day with her. Jeff's impression—and he is right—was that his appearance lifted a burden from her heart. She told him, I don't know why she let you go. We would have found a way.

Of course Jeff wanted to know about his father, too, but Frieda was no help. She thought Edith had dated a lieutenant from Chicago, but she didn't know anything about him, not even his name. The pregnancy had been a complete surprise (again!) to her, and Edith had refused to say anything at all about the father. She had made all the adoption arrangements through a lawyer before the baby was born, and when she came home from the hospital, she told her mother, if you ever mention this to anyone, I'll take Sandra away.

Mae, who had slept in a bed with Edith, tells me she had no idea Edith had a baby. Edith was small and never vigorous; when her tummy bulged, not so very much, she mentioned that she might have a tumor. She told the neighbors about it, how eventually when the doctors figured it out, she went to the hospital, had surgery, came home and got better. All of that story would be hard for me to believe, except that when I was at college in Austin, a girl who lived in the room downstairs from me went home at Christmas and had a baby. None of us—including her roommate—had had any idea she had been pregnant.

I'm sorry that Jeff had nowhere to look for his birth father, and I'm sorry that he had no explanation for his mother's decision to let another family raise him. Maybe there had been a soldier who shipped out; maybe something worse. But I think that what mattered was that she thought another child would tie her to her mother and she would never get away. She didn't feel strong enough for another baby; never mind that it was mostly her sister and mother who took care of me. Frieda had to have wept for the baby, but she would have seen the rejection another way, too, as a deeply cruel insult to her. In some way, I feel the same; it seems as if, after two years with me, she would have welcomed another child. Easy to say now. She was nineteen.

But there is this: Jeff grew to adulthood in a stable home with parents. (Not a mile from Frieda's house. At one time he was her paper boy.)

Within a few months, Edith met a sweet chubby eighteen-year-old Yankee boy who had enlisted in the Air Force, been sent to Sheppard Air Force Base, and almost as soon as he had mastered the square corner on his cot, was discharged like thousands of other latecomers.

So Edith married Dean Hupp and brought him home to that crowded little box of a house. She might have already been pregnant, or she got pregnant right away, and the couple headed to Ohio—an episode in all our lives that Frieda was willing to discuss with me after Edith died and Dean was long gone and good riddance.

Frieda hated Dean the minute she met him. The couple had "eloped" at the justice of the peace office, and Edith called to say, I'm bringing my husband home. Frieda made fried chicken that first evening, and he took a wing and the back, like she might not let him have a thigh. She asked him to help her fix a loose board on the front porch, and he said sure, if you show me what to do. She told me, Edith just put her hand in a bag and pulled him out. When did she have time to meet him? What was the damned hurry?

He still had baby fat, a loopy grin; he was shy and ignorant; he had no skills and no education. Frieda couldn't understand why the Air Force had let him in. Edith insisted that he look into programs at Midwestern University, but Frieda made it clear she was not taking on another dependent. He couldn't see himself in college anyway. Since he got out of high school one year earlier things had been hopping, and he wanted to take Edith away so they could start their own life.

All he knew to do was to go home and let his daddy find him a job. What a day the departure must have been—an old car spitting exhaust, Mother staring straight ahead, and me in the back seat, looking through the window, screaming Mommy, Mommy, long after North Lamar was out of sight.

Of course, as Frieda knew, it was a mistake. Edith and Dean had hardly arrived in Ohio before Edith wrote: I'm sick with this pregnancy. I can hardly keep my head up. I can't handle her. (I was famous for my temper tantrums.) Frieda went up on the train to fetch me and took me home to Wichita Falls where, I presume, I had plenty of attention from her and Mae (who was pregnant, too, staying with Frieda).

After Edith had the baby, Dean got a job in Martins Ferry, Ohio. Edith wrote to say it wasn't right for me to be away from her, and so she and the baby would take the train to Wichita Falls and take me back to Martins Ferry.

Frieda wrote:

> I have had you on my mind all day. I feel like something is wrong with someone & it is likely to be you.
>
> Edith, I don't believe you should make a trip on the train. If he can't bring you in a car, if you will pay for my fare, I will bring her home, as bad as I hate to. I will not stay even a day for I can't stand to leave her after she gets there.
>
> Edith, Sandra throws the awfulest fits of temper & we can't do a thing with her, & if she was to have one on the train when you have Karen to take care of, I don't know how you'd make it.
>
> Hope you and Hubba Hubba are doing okay. Will send some peas when I can find some, probably canned though.
>
> Bye bye love.

She went on to apologize for not having cash for a ticket. She had finally put a little money into her house, painting the kitchen and laying linoleum, and she had to borrow for that. She was hoping that Sonny would go on with school (he was a month away from being sixteen), but by fall he would be in the Army.

The same week, Frieda's mother, Tillie, wrote Edith from Devol, Oklahoma, to express the same worries about a trip being too much for her. And, coincidentally, Tillie had painted her kitchen recently, too—a green color that she liked but "nobody else seems too [*sic*]," which could only have meant her husband and her brother, both men given to slight nods when words weren't absolutely necessary. She backed up the assessment of my behavior too:

> Sandra is sure getting spoiled. I think she practically runs Wichita. I notice they can't do much with her if she don't want to. I don't see how you could make a trip with a little baby by yourself and then Sandra too.

She enclosed five dollars for Edith "to do whatever you want with," and mentioned that she bought a size three-month dress for Karen. It's nice to see a bit of humor too. The gas man had been out and said the kitchen "looks lovely." Then the hail insurance man came out and he said, this is a very pretty looking kitchen, ma'am. Tillie comments, No I'm not flirting with the gas or insurance men, it was volentary [*sic*]. (Along with the hailstorm troubles, they had recently had a "skunk attack" and stayed home from church for three weeks until she could get the smell out of their good clothes.)

It makes me happy to read these letters, to feel the intimacy and support for my mother, so far away. As much as Frieda didn't like Dean, his parents felt the same way about Edith. North and South? Who knows? Edith's life was taking shape with "Hubba Hubba" (Frieda never said his name), but it must have been hard to have a baby without her family around. Independence had a lot of loneliness in it. I guess when I arrived she was comforted to have her two girls together with her. And there was something else: it wasn't long before she wrote to Jack in New Mexico and asked him if he would want to come and see her some time. She would have wanted me there for him to see.

I bet Frieda didn't know anything about that.

* * *

Ten years after Frieda died, my aunt wrote Jack and told him about me. She sent clippings about my books and photographs of my daughter and me. She realized she didn't have to keep a secret just because her mother did, but she wanted to save me from disappointment, so she left it in his hands. It took him a couple months to decide, and then he called me, not long after my fiftieth birthday. There were phone calls, letters, photographs exchanged. I flew to New Mexico. He cried in the airport. I'd know you anywhere, he said. She was the love of my life. I'd have married her. I'd have died for her.

It seemed so sad, so poignant, so perfectly brought to this moment. Never mind his six children or his wife, long lost to Alzheimer's. I was giddy. I felt lucky to know, at last. My aunt was thrilled; he's very successful, she told me.

A young Hopi woman at the hospital took our blood for DNA tests. Jack was jubilant when the results confirmed our kinship. He introduced me to people all over Gallup, including his priest. He told his kids to get used to me.

He never said anything about having seen me in Ohio, an encounter that as of yet I knew nothing about. It would be several years after we met before a scrap from my mother's diary that I found stuck among some photographs made me realize he had visited Edith, had seen me, and then had gone away, never to be heard from again. It's just a scrap of paper, but it feels heavy when I hold it.

I was angry when I found my mother's note about Jack: *He wants us.* Because he hadn't wanted us. I was a living doll, but he was impervious. He felt no responsibility for me; another man was my father. I sent him a photocopy of Edith's note, and suddenly other issues rose up between us. What was logical didn't matter to me (Edith had been married, with another child.). All I could think about was my mother's fantasy of a different life, and her pain. And he said he had forgotten! I felt gutted. I'd lost two fathers, now.

In time, we corresponded again, then talked. After a few years I saw him again; it no longer seemed necessary to resolve anything. He loves me. He is an old man, a good man, and I am better off for knowing him. There isn't any way to fix the past, and no good reason to suffer it.

What Jack found in Ohio was a hot burner he wouldn't touch. Everything with Edith was too complicated. Anyone could understand that. He drove away and did the sensible thing. But what made me so angry was that he didn't think to tell her he would never be back. He forgot her. He forgot me. I was haunted by the thought of her hoping, then losing hope, turning back to the reality of her choices. I bet he still has the copy of her note. I regret now that I sent it to him, not because of the anger I felt, but because I begrudge him the sentimental satisfaction I imagine him feeling when he saw the artifact of his romantic youth.

He wants us, my mother, the love of his life, wrote in her diary. *He says he will come for us. Life can finally begin.*

Soon after Jack's stopover, Edith and Dean and their two girls piled in a junk car and made the trip to Wichita Falls. Mae had found a new husband, and Sonny had gone to Italy with the Army, so the back bedroom in Frieda's house was empty.

I don't know what Dean was feeling when they left the Midwest or when they arrived in Texas, though I can guess. I think both Edith and Frieda were happy, though, each needing the other. As for me, I was home.

In 1954, in Odessa, Edith was feeling okay. She had down days, but most of the time she was up and busy. My sister was in school, so Edith could do what she liked during the days. She didn't like the priest at the Catholic parish, so she worshiped with the Mexicans in a Quonset hut across town.

There was a trailer with three tiny religious Sisters from Mexico living there. They visited the sick, took care of the priest's house and meals, and ran a little daycare center for the children of Mexican mothers who had to work. Edith loved everybody. She learned basic Spanish quickly. In the summer, when I was home, she took my sister and me there during the day. Usually we went early for Mass, and I played a small organ. There was a little boy, David, a toddler still in diapers. His mother had died, and the father was having a hard time taking care of the boy. Edith said she would take him home with her during the week. It was an informal arrangement, not very well thought-out, but it was a relief for the boy's father, and the child was a joy for my mother. Typically, Dean had no opinion. He was working in the oilfields fifty hours a week or more. When he was home he wanted to sleep.

Before long the child lived full time with them, and his father said if she wanted, Edith could adopt him. These things take time, but David was there all through the months I was in eighth grade, when I boarded with the religious Sisters in Wichita Falls.

At Christmas, we had a piñata. Edith had bought a rocking horse for David. I don't remember any of my gifts; in fact, I don't remember any of my Christmas presents, ever, though I had them.

Frieda came by with presents on her way home from Mae's house. When she saw the situation, she was beside herself. She told Edith she wasn't well enough to take care of a baby. (A Mexican baby! She didn't say that.) What if she got sick again? Who would look after him then? My mother said God would work things out. The papers made their way through the courts; it was all just paperwork, a poor couple adopting a poor baby.

But before David would have become an official part of my family, his mother's aunt came up from Mexico and took him home with her. I thought my mother would die of it. She went to bed for months. I think by then my little sister was raising herself, taking what she could get.

I'm sure Mother loved David, but I'm also sure she had not forgotten the child she left behind in the hospital for someone else to claim. She must have thought how she would have loved him, too, and nobody would have taken him away; she should have known. She must have wondered at the irony of her going on to have another baby after him so quickly.

But the pain right then was for David. I have such a vivid memory of her squatting down, one hand on David's back, while with her other hand she wiped his face clean. Little one, she would say to him. Precious boy.

Frieda didn't tell that story to Jeff, but I did. She told him Edith was young and scared and selfish when she was pregnant that second time. She hadn't known what she would do with two babies. She never knew how she was going to feel. She would never find a husband.

She didn't want to ask her mother to help her on and on. She wanted her child to have a better home than she could give him. She meant well, and maybe she hadn't known how hard it would be, how much it would hurt. She didn't know how marriage would disappoint her, or how quickly she would be back in her mother's house. The lost baby was the price of something she never had.

My daughter gave birth to her daughter in a padded plastic tub in her bed-room in January 2009. The midwife had filled the tub with warm water from a hose that snaked down the hallway to a bathroom spigot. I was there and so was my dog. I rode the rhythm of my daughter's labor, held my breath as the baby's head appeared, plunged my arms in to receive her. While the midwives tended my daughter, I took the baby to a bed in another room and laid her on my naked chest. She sucked my little finger.

I had not dared hope for a grandchild. For so long my daughter had had her hands full taking care of herself. But here she is, this child named for my mother, sturdy and stubborn and beautiful.

I stayed with them the whole first year, and most of the second. Edie called me Mommy—spontaneously, I swear!—until she went to preschool. There the teachers corrected her: that's your grandma. So she calls me Gramma-Mommy.

When my daughter was born, I felt caught up in a dream in which she was me, and I was Edith, mothering her but also mothering myself. When Edie was born, I felt an uncanny sense of Frieda's presence in me. As I fell in love with Edie I knew what it was to have had Frieda's love; maybe, maybe, also what it had been like to be her. That is what I want for Edith Jane: the sweetness of childhood, the confidence of being loved. I want to live long enough for her to remember me, uncomplicatedly.

MOMMY

LUCKY DUCK

A lot of the past is sad.

So it seems really important to make myself clear. I was a happy little girl. I was a lucky duck. Until we moved out of Frieda's house the summer I turned ten, I was the princess, and the house on North Lamar was my castle.

I don't have any memories of the time before Edith married Dean, so he was always Daddy to me until she died, when Frieda could stop pretending he was my father, and he could start all over in his life; he was only thirty-one years old. I remember leaving for Ohio when I was three, but nothing past the turn on the street, away from my grandmother's house. My remembered life starts at four, and I was very much at home in my grandmother's house. I'm convinced there is another kind of memory, though, visceral and deep-rooted, that goes with a child as she grows up: it is the subconscious awareness of having been loved at the start. I certainly knew Frieda loved me. And all my childhood, my aunt was another extension of my sense of home and kinship. When I was in her house—every summer, usually for a month at a time—I wasn't visiting. I lived there. After Edith died, though, I never again felt at home with Dean. He was never unkind; I don't think his disappearance from my life was deliberate so much as careless. I was with Edith's kin, and he wanted nothing to do with any of them. And he finally had a healthy, lusty wife; how could Edith's kids compete with that?

Consider my homecoming from the hospital on that scorching August day in 1943. My very first ride in a taxicab. Frieda's squat adobe house. The swamp cooler is pumping air through its wet wads, everything is spick and span, there's no end to the cooing and exclaiming at my arrival. Sonny is thirteen years old, a sweet kid itching to be old enough to go to war. Mae is sixteen, learning to be a medical lab technician at her high school. She is jealous of Edith for lots of reasons but crazy about her baby, on the spot. Edith has just turned eighteen. She is wan and wary and eager to lie down, so she hands the baby over to her mother and goes straight to bed. Frieda has fretted for months, wondering if Edith is strong enough for childbirth; she didn't know how they were going to stuff another person, child or not, into her little box of a house. But when Edith hands me to her, that's that. Relief, love. She knows she is going to be responsible for me, and she is glad. Of course I was bottle-fed, so anyone could manage that. I know my aunt took care of me a lot when she wasn't in school, but flesh to flesh, it was Frieda who felt like mother. I started calling her Mommy before I could say anything else at all.

The house, built in 1934, was yellow stucco with a flat roof. It had a concrete slab porch that had settled at a tilt. If you stood at the front door you could look straight through the back one, through the living room and the kitchen and the closed-in back porch used for storage. Two small bedrooms were along one side, with a bathroom in between. The lot the house stood on was huge, 7,000 square feet of bare dirt and patchy weeds sloping down to the unpaved street that flooded in spring rains. The alley at the back of the lot had mud holes after it rained, perfect spots to look for tadpoles.

The sisters shared a bed in the back of the house. A small second-hand crib was set up on Edith's side. Sonny slept in the living room on a cot padded with quilts, near the only source of heat in the house, a big brown metal gas stove. There was a radio in the kitchen. There was a "wiener dog," Tiny, who followed Frieda around like a shadow and would live to be very old.

Edith and Mae doted on me, but I wanted Frieda. I howled when she left the house. I slept in her bed when she worked at night. I followed her around like Tiny did.

And when we went to Ohio, and from there, to Indiana, I cried for her, day in and day out, until my mother finally wrote to Frieda and said, please, please come get her. I can't remember that time, though sometimes images flicker and I think: I do remember. The dog that knocked me down in the street. My mother draining clabber through a cheesecloth. My sister in her crib.

Within the year, we were all in Frieda's house again. It wasn't what Edith had had in mind, but Dean had lost his job, and besides, she needed help with her children.

I know that my mother suffered in those years, but I don't really remember much of that. I was my grandmother's angel, my uncle's kiddo, my aunt's precious, my mother's darling. I remember library books and crayon drawings, playing outside until deep dusk, jump rope and sandbox and hop-scotch, the stuff of a fifties childhood. The family next door had daughters the same ages as my sister and I, and their mother was a good friend to Frieda and Edith. There was always someone to pay attention to me when I wanted that, and nobody worried when I wanted to be outdoors. Kids played outside all up and down the street. And when it got too hot, we kids put a quilt down on the floor in front of the swamp cooler and slept until supper.

I remember grocery shopping with Frieda. I went with her to the laundromat; in fair weather she brought the wet clothes home to hang on a line. The first chore I ever learned was folding towels. The second was cleaning the lavatory sink, and I didn't progress much after that.

We went to the farm in Devol at least every other weekend for the day, or sometimes, in summer, on Friday evening, returning on Sunday afternoon. We parked in the dusty yard near the water tank and went into the house by way of a concrete porch that ran the width of the house. It was always the same: I ran into the house to hug Rightmama. (I had so many "Mamas," I called them special names: Frieda was Mommy; Edith was Mama, and because Frieda called Tillie Mama, I did, too, until I got frustrated at the confusion—Edith and Tillie having the same names—and I insisted that Tillie was the *right* Mama. It stuck, for me and for all the kids to come.)

Next I checked to see what the pies were. She would have baked that morning and set the pies out on the counter with flour sacks covering them. Custard or lemon meringue pies went in the refrigerator, and that was the first place I looked. I loved the lemon, and sometimes—if it was at least two hours before lunch—I would get a piece right off.

The house was always spotless. The living room, where I never once saw anyone sit, looked like a parlor on a movie set. There was a player piano, and we could play it if we didn't go on too long. Rightmama's bedroom, directly off the kitchen, was more or less off bounds except for naps. Daddy Hill's room opened onto the dining room, and no one minded if I played under his bed.

There were all the things you'd expect on a farm: the outhouse; chickens hopping about, pecking for feed; a henhouse; a barn with a hayloft—I never went up there, because the hay was scratchy, and I was afraid of critters. In front of the house (the back was the real entrance) there were three rows of poplars, the house being the fourth line of a square. Sometimes we sought shade out there but never stayed for long; there was nothing to do or see.

All the women were in the kitchen, which took up a third of the house. There was a gas stove, a rocker, chairs, a small table, and often a quilting rack. After noontime dinner on Sunday, someone would get out the dominoes or cards. Meanwhile, kids just did whatever they wanted until it was time to go or time to sleep. Frieda's sister's kids, older than me by five and six years, kept comic books in a closet, where there was a light and enough room to close yourself inside while you read. I would never have asked to buy a comic book. I was too snobbish about books. I read them though, with guilty pleasure.

You never knew who might show up. In the summer Frieda's sister, Frances, who was a math teacher, stayed at least a month with her kids, turning the parlor into a makeshift bedroom. Mae brought her kids off and on in the summer, which she spent mostly at her in-laws' house in Wichita Falls. Once in a while one of Frieda's brothers would drop by with his wife, and there were other relatives on Rightmama's side, too. Her brother, Albert, who had been the baby of her family, lived with the Hills for decades until his death. He had a bed and a chest on a closed-in, uninsulated porch   and a lot of blankets.

Mae's in-laws, the Perkins, acted as if my sister and I were just another couple of grandkids, and we spent many days at their house when Mae and our cousins were there. We couldn't run or make noise indoors, but we didn't really want to be in the house anyway. The Perkins property had a beautiful green lawn and lots of shade. It was like our private park. I was the oldest cousin by three years, so I spent a lot of time by myself, reading. I got lots of indulgent teasing remarks: smarty-pants, show off, head-in-a-book. Later in the summer we would all drive to Mae's house, wherever Halliburton took them: Big Spring, Midland, Hadacol Corner—now Midkiff, Kermit. I never wondered what my mother was doing while I was in West Texas. Away from her, I couldn't call up her image. I wonder now what it was like for her. A relief, I suppose; she could give herself over to the pain and lassitude. I hope she didn't feel guilty or lonely. She knew we kids had fun at her sister's house.

Daddy—Dean—came and went, changing jobs frequently, working days then nights. Mother had a run of good health and worked on Democrat Ralph Yarborough's senatorial campaign before she fell ill again. I sold Campfire Girls candy and rode a bus back and forth to Catholic school. I took ballet lessons and learned to dance en pointe. At Christmas we drove to the rich part of town to see the lights display on the property of the Burnses, a wealthy oil baron and his wife. It was a fabulous show, and we were wowed. It never crossed my mind to wonder why their house was so big and ours was so small.

And all that time, Frieda, my Mommy, worked at General Mills, packing flour. She never talked about work. She never stayed home sick.

There was drama in the household: worries about Sonny in the service and Edith's illnesses; times when Dean had no work and got hard looks from his mother-in-law. But it all went right past me. When Frieda took me to see the house she was building across town on Grant Street, that spring when I was nine, I assumed that we would all move there. I thought it would be fun to start over in a new house. It was bleak out there, flat land stretching beyond the houses, and I never saw any kids around, but we would all be together; that was all that mattered.

Right up until they were packing, none of the grown-ups thought to tell me my world was about to split in two. It was time for my family to be in our own home. I know that now, but I didn't know it then.

I cried a lot, but then I got my first bicycle and rode every day on the wide, flat paved streets all around the housing complex. My sister and I shared a bedroom and our parents had theirs. There were silverfish on the walls, and the concrete floors were frigid, but my parents relished their privacy. We listened to radio programs—*People Are Funny*, *Our Miss Brooks*, *Mr. and Mrs. North*. In the depth of winter, Mother drove me to the Boys Club for swimming lessons. Frieda came now and then with a bag of groceries. If Dean was there, he went in the bedroom. She and Edith sat at the kitchen table and spoke in low voices, never for very long. I followed her out to her car, where we could kiss and hold on for a minute. It would be months before I would go to her house, almost a year before I spent the night there. She had her house, and now we had ours.

thought my mother was mean to her mother and to me. I don't know what I think now. Certainly I have more empathy than I did as a child, but a buried resentment bubbles in me: how could she have kept me from Frieda? How was it better for me to be lonely than for her to give in—to what, I don't know. Frieda never spoke a word of criticism of Edith to me.

As soon as we moved out of her house and got settled, Edith started working as a carhop at a Pig Stand Drive-In. She was saving money so that we could all go to Ohio to see Dean's family. She showed Frieda the fringed jackets and boots she had bought for my sister and me. Frieda told her she was asking to be sick. Edith had complained about her in laws, and now she was wearing herself out to go see them. It didn't make sense. She asked her, why doesn't Hubba Hubba go see his folks alone? She told her, your car won't get you as far as Kansas.

She had borrowed money for our trip. She told me it was insurance, in case something went wrong. She gave it to me for safekeeping. It was our secret, and I could give it back to her if it wasn't needed. What could be more sensible? I didn't wonder why Frieda didn't give the money to my mother. When I think about it now, I suppose she was afraid that if she gave it to Edith, Edith would refuse it. Or maybe it was a talisman: if I carried the money, we wouldn't need it. Surely she meant to help and protect us.

When the car broke down half a day from home and my parents moaned to think what it would cost them and what would we do while it was getting fixed, I felt like Superman flying to vanquish the villain. The thing about feelings, we all know, is that they aren't anything like clear thinking and practical judgment. The only thing my parents could have done was call

Frieda; she would have had to wire them money. It would have been humil-
iating and their gratitude would have been grudging; Frieda wouldn't have
said a word, but I told you so would have been like a banner across the
sky. This way, though, it was worse; something I could not comprehend.
Frieda had been sure they would have trouble with their old car; she had
been right, and she had entrusted her assistance to a child. I thought I was
a hero. My mother thought I was a traitor, "siding" with Frieda. I didn't
understand what they were so upset about. Now I can see why Edith was
insulted, especially because Frieda involved me deviously, but I also understand that my grandmother was right to worry. Frieda should have worked
out her "insurance" with Edith, but that's saying that Edith should have
appreciated her mother's concern. Therein lay the problem. There have
been enough times when I saw what was coming as a consequence of my
daughter's decisions for me to grasp just how hard it is to stand by, or if
you don't, for the child to feel appreciation instead of resentment. It's not
that the mother is right; it's that the child is wrong. Again. It's easy enough
to say, they have to suffer the consequences; it's a lot harder to turn away
from the train wreck you see coming, especially when, in the end, you are
sure you will have to pick up the pieces.

Dean was a good worker, and construction was booming. He took a job
building patios, which were suddenly so popular. Less than a year after
we moved into the project, we moved again to a house on a pretty street.
We got a dog, a part-Scottie mutt. My sister named her Blackie. We had a
backyard with grass and a stone fence that was flat on top so I could play
tightrope walker. My sister and I had a long walk to and from school—the
Academy of Mary Immaculate—past shops and a drugstore, houses and
a park; in winter, we took a bus. There were lots of kids on the block. Most
days, Edith wasn't feeling too sick. She had all day to rest.

I was secretary of my class.

I talked to Frieda on the phone every week, but I minded less and less that I wasn't seeing her. I loved school, and I loved our home and the neighborhood. I remember the summer of 1954 as the best time we ever had as a family.

Then Dean tried to start his own business, making concrete blocks for patio construction. He had learned to make them while working for a contractor, and there was a demand for the product. His boss, who had a lot of work, encouraged him, saying he would be glad to cut the production out of his own business so he could just concentrate on building patios; he would be Dean's best customer. The mistake Dean made was to partner with a black man who had worked for the same contractor. They couldn't get credit. They couldn't get supplies. They couldn't conduct business. The old boss shrugged; he couldn't intercede with suppliers. Things might have worked out if the black man were hired by Dean as a laborer, but as partners, they were sunk. I remember going to the partner's home; Edith liked his wife. I wonder why Dean didn't just say he was sorry and go out on his own; he never seemed like a radical man, though he could be stubborn. But Edith would have resisted the split and encouraged Dean's sense of outrage. He went to his old boss to ask for work, but his job was filled.

He started selling Watkins products door to door in the evenings, while he went around the city day after day, trying to get what he needed to start production of the blocks. The electrician who lived up the street, a nice man who gave us kids rides in his pickup bed through the cemetery after work, took Dean aside. He was a friendly man, a fair man, too, he said. People are talking, he said. It's how it is. You can't fight it. Look where you live.

Edith had to borrow money from her mother. Dean finally did what Frieda and Mae had been after him to do for years. He went to Dallas to apply for a job with Halliburton. Uncle Howard, Mae's husband, called to put in a word. Dean was hired right away and moved without us to Odessa.

Edith stayed in Wichita Falls for some months after, while Dean lived in a rented room in the house of a widow of a Halliburton man. But the time came when he had saved money for a deposit on a house and enough to move his family. What a quandary for Frieda. Dean finally had a steady job, and it would take Edith away from her. It would take me away.

Only I didn't go. The Sisters pleaded with my mother to let me stay on as a boarder. I was a prize student; they would take good care of me. My mother could send a little money when she had it. One day she dropped me off at the school, then drove away with my sister while I stood on the steps, too stunned to wave. I realized the dog wasn't with them.

The dormitory was on the top floor, across the hall from the typing room, where I learned the keyboard from a chart on the wall. There were ten or so of us. We all slept in the one long room, pulling white curtains around our beds at night. There were two large bathrooms—one with toilets, the other with tubs. The other boarders were older girls from small towns or farms who went home every weekend. From Friday evening until Sunday afternoon, I was the only one left. On Saturdays, I helped the young novices clean—I worked up to dusting the chapel pews. One of them ate lunch with me; a different one ate supper with me. I practiced the piano in a downstairs parlor and read piles of books: *The Royal Road to Romance. The Unwilling Vessel. Ben Hur. Therese, the Little Flower of Lisieux.* Often the Mistress of Boarders gave me money to go across the street to get a hamburger. Sometimes after Mass on Sunday a parish family took me to lunch with them. I liked to sit in the beautiful chapel. I thought about becoming a nun; I'd want to be in a contemplative order, like the Carmelites. I'd want it to be hard, so that I would be extra holy.

Frieda was just across town, but I never saw her. I wanted to spend weekends with her, but when I asked the Mistress of Boarders, she said my mother was very clear that I was to stay at the school. I talked to Frieda on the pay phone in the basement, and she said, your mother has the say. Nobody ever suggested a reason for this banishment of my grandmother, my sentence of separation from her. It might have been as minor as an offhand remark from Frieda at the time of the move. It might have been an accumulation of grudges. Edith had established her authority over her life by asserting her authority over mine. I didn't think it was fair. I still don't. I could have spent every weekend with my grandmother, but my mother wouldn't hear of it.

When I called her, I tried to think of interesting things to tell her, though all I really wanted was to keep the connection open as long as possible. She began coming to the school grounds during my lunch hour recess several times a week when she wasn't working days. She would stand at the cyclone fence at the far corner of the block; I would run over to kiss her, reach over the fence to touch her, speak for a few moments, and then run back. She usually gave me a dollar, despite my protests that I had nothing to spend it on (only peanuts and Dr. Pepper in Sister Adelaide's basement candy shop). When Frieda appeared, the playground monitor, one of the younger Sisters, always turned her back and busied herself with other girls. In bad weather, Frieda drove around the block, and I watched the car from a basement window. It was something we had agreed on when winter set in. It sounds pathetic now, but I know she wanted me to know that she was *there*; if I really needed her, I could brave the cold; I could run to the fence. I could count on her.

The next year Edith relented. I was allowed to go to Frieda's house every month or so. It was blissful: a soft bed, a long hot bath, food I chose, television. She didn't come to my piano recital, though; she didn't come to my graduation. She had a corsage delivered for my recital. Other students had parents and aunts and uncles, cousins and friends. Frieda said it wasn't a good idea for her to come; she didn't think she would be welcome. All I could say was, that's stupid! I didn't think how it must have felt to be her, to have my time with her doled out by oddly dressed women who didn't even know her. I couldn't imagine the Sisters saying one unkind word to her, if they noticed her at all, and graduation was going to be in church, for heaven's sake, but she was implacable. It's your occasion, she said about each event. It's too bad your mother can't be here.

She knew I would be leaving at the end of the year and wouldn't come back to Wichita Falls. Maybe she was practicing being without me. Maybe she was weary. Or wary. Or maybe she, too, had a streak of spite to play out through me. Sure enough, Edith asked me: Did Mommy come?

My face burned at the question. I said, you knew she wouldn't.

PIXIE DUST

t was the last week of May 1965. I had just finished a school year of teaching at the Catholic academy in Wichita Falls. I had lived with my grandmother all year, and I was desperate to get away. We cried and hugged as I packed my car, but I had come to the house straight from turning in my grades, ready to go, and no amount of reasoning (it would be better to start early tomorrow; you must be tired, you should rest a few days; what's the rush?) would delay my departure. I was twenty-one years old, and I couldn't spend another hour in my grandmother's house. It's time, I kept thinking. It's time to be on my own.

I threw my bag and my typewriter into the back seat of my Volkswagen, promised to call when I arrived at my destination, and drove away without looking back. I knew I would find a job—I could type. I crossed the state line into Oklahoma, and a huge sense of relief and adventure and freedom welled up in me as I headed for Chicago, where a friend was living. I felt myself expanding.

I suppose it's natural for a young adult to feel trapped, as I did, when she has failed to begin a mature life. What felt like escape was merely moving on. I thought that my grandmother had been glad for my company, and I had tried to show her that I was grateful. For months I was comforted by the coziness and safety of her home and her company. I knew she was proud of my teaching. Then during Christmas break, I went to Mexico—I knew she disapproved, but I didn't care—and in the new year there were bouts of tension, heavy as thunderclouds, that stirred up a childish anguish in me over my dependence. Her moodiness mostly had to do with Sonny, who was so unhappy and having a terrible time holding a job. He had a wife and four children; his temper tantrums and walk-offs from jobs—his pride—were an indulgence he could not afford. She warned him and he ignored her; she helped him, and he didn't pay her back. He looked like his father but had none of Ira's joyfulness. If he'd stayed in the Army, he'd be retiring now. If he hadn't gone in the Army, he'd be a healthier man. If he was ever going to hold a job, he had to learn to keep his mouth shut. He came and went, always mad, and Frieda bristled with anger and anxiety. Sonny had leased a long haul truck that year, but he hated driving, or the truck was a lemon, or there weren't enough trips. His back was killing him, and his wife couldn't handle the boys by herself. On and on. He parked the truck right in front of Frieda's house, mostly in her yard, where it sat for months until someone came in the night and drove it away.

There was nothing I could say or do to make things better; it was like breathing smoke. I thought, this is why people get divorced. I made such a small Catholic school salary that I couldn't have rented my own apartment, and besides, the whole point was to save money for later. (I wanted to go to Greece.) Anyway, it would have hurt her if I had lived somewhere else in the city.

Though she never criticized me, I felt defensive. Surely, I thought, she was weary of bailing me out. I thought all the time about my inevitable departure, and I assumed she thought about it, too. After all, in the year between college and my arrival at her door, I had been in New York, California, and Mexico, sometimes going two or three months without sending so much as a postcard to her.

The house was so small that we couldn't avoid brushing one another or stepping aside, a movement that always felt insulting. I wouldn't have dreamed of saying, let's talk about it. What was "it," anyway? We kept our thoughts to ourselves. I did the laundry (this required tedious trips to the laundromat but gave me time out of the house) and often cooked. I took her out to Luby's Cafeteria on my payday. We watched Johnny Carson together. If she laughed, I laughed too and moved over closer to her. I wondered why it felt okay between us one day but not the other. Now I can look back and see that mostly it was good, being there with her, but when things were tense, it felt as if it was always so. In my own way, I was replaying my mother's experience, allowing my neediness to fold into resentment.

A few times I sputtered out something about my mother. I wanted to know what she was like as a girl. I wanted to know what she was like with me when I was a baby. I wanted to say I missed her. Frieda deflected my timid questions with a sigh or a small sad shake of her head. The message was clear: I can't talk about her.

In the living room, on a shelf, there was a photograph of Edith—a small black-and-white picture of her face. She would be dead within a month of when it was taken, and yet, surprisingly, she is still pretty. A little puffy. Drawn on eyebrows (she lost hers to anesthesia in her twenties), short bleached hair. Her gaze is intelligent, pensive, wishful, and melancholy. It is full of her. That must be why my grandmother framed it, but I never got over my amazement that she had. The picture was cut out of a photograph of her nude, taken by a neighbor who was a studio photographer and trying his hand at "art." I always wondered: how could my grandmother forget for even the briefest glance that the picture was part of a larger, more shocking one? How could she not consider what I, Edith's daughter, must think? (She saved the nude pictures; they came to me. Last year I destroyed them. I wasn't ashamed of them, but I didn't want anyone else to see them. I didn't want there to be even the smallest chance that someone might judge her.)

Maybe Frieda liked the picture because of the way my mother's eyes always seemed to be looking at you as you looked at her. Maybe she recognized true things in the picture, or maybe it was just that it was the last photograph. It was strange to me that there were no other pictures of Edith, neither of her as a child, nor of me as a child with her. I didn't ask where my mother's photographs were or what photos Frieda had. There were boxes in my room, in my closet, in the storage shed in the backyard. It was clear that Frieda wanted to keep things from the past, and just as clear that she couldn't bear to look at them. It's funny to look back. I thought of myself as some kind of rebel, but I was too timid to ask: What's this? Where's that? What are you feeling?

* * *

I was depressed about the blankness of my future. I had a bachelor's degree from the University of Texas, but I didn't feel I had learned much. Certainly, teaching in a Catholic school for $250 a month while living with my grandmother was a stopgap. I didn't have a teaching certificate. No one had ever talked to me about my future. I had no idea how the world was run. I couldn't have named five vocations. Nurse? Actress? I had applied to American Airlines and the Peace Corps—what a joke—and though I was stung by the rejections I received, though I cried into my pillow and longed to talk, I couldn't imagine that Frieda would understand. She had labored her whole life, while I had had the privilege of an education. The trouble was, the privilege had been one big rush, accumulating course credits almost randomly, with no idea what an education was. The experience—forty-eight credits in one year of community college, then two years in the baffling universe of a major university—had been rife with misjudgment, misdeed, and devaluation.

And my grief about my mother had not gone away. Her death was a big hole we tiptoed around. Frieda had saved every scrap she could rescue of my mother's belongings—she even had her refrigerator, beside her own—but what she knew about her, what she felt, was inaccessible to me.

It simply didn't occur to me that the pain I was enduring was no more than what she felt, too, what she had felt for a much longer time about other deaths, and that for all her life she had borne, suppressed, and ultimately denied the power of all that grief. Was she withholding to save the rest of us from her sorrow, or was it just none of our business? If we had talked about our feelings, it would have been like opening the door to a fierce wind, but so much doubt and tension could have been resolved. We would have known one another in a deeper way. Because we didn't, I wanted to flee the pressure of what was unsaid. I was suffocating.

I think of her grief as pixie dust—a silent, constant, invisible shower that fell on her family. There was always something wrong. We needed her, but nobody wants to be a grown-up and still a child, too. We wanted to get away from her. I thought that was how the world worked. There was no peace, no place to settle. Men and women made compromised alliances and then struggled within them. I wanted to live by myself. I didn't want to fall in love or have children. I didn't know how to find tolerable, sufficient work. I had been a smarty-pants in school, but now I felt stupid. I didn't know what I wanted, and I was sure I couldn't get it. Life had already taught me what Frieda knew best: our family's geography was built on karst. Sink-holes everywhere.

The boxes in my kitchen cupboard seemed to emit a pulsating beacon. I dreamed about my mother and my grandmother every night. I anguished over all the questions I could not answer: How did my grandmother bear her husband's death? What was Mother thinking when she went to California, pregnant with me? How had my mother's death shaped my life? Later I would take a direct avenue and write a memoir about my mother, *Occasions of Sin*, and of course, eventually, I would write about Frieda, but in 1995, when I began to write *Plain Seeing*, I wanted to write a fictional narrative from the cloth of family mystery. It would be both discovery and escape.

I decided that I would use a two-part structure. The first half of the novel would be about my mother's childhood and young adulthood—the death of her father, her dreams of a better life, her pregnancy. Because I was writing fiction, I could write a cohesive story without being bound to what really happened. The essential truth was only this: a girl wanted a bigger life than the one she was granted, but in the end she lived a familiar one, pregnant, unmarried, and dependent on her mother. It sounded sad, but I was determined to make it romantic.

I read voraciously about farms and movies and train stations. I visited Gallup, where the family had lived for a year and where my mother had worked in a railroad restaurant and had her brief relationship with the father of her child. To me it was an exotic setting. I even took a train ride down the length of California especially to spend a long layover in the grand Los Angeles train station. I was determined to give Edith, now Emma Laura, the romance with life she surely did not have. I gave her a tiny role in a movie—a moment of triumph and hope.

In the second half of the novel, I wanted to pursue these questions: What happens when a woman cannot let go of grief for her dead mother? How does her obsession affect her ability to live a present life? I didn't want the novel to be about me, except for the impulse to explore those questions. So I decided to have Emma Laura's daughter, Lucy, grow up and marry a wealthy man from the East Coast. The trajectory of her life would be nothing like my own, but I could draw on memories to feed the undercurrent of loss, especially the frustration of having questions with no answers. I also realized that I had created a new mystery. Was the story of Emma Laura the one that her daughter Lucy could never know? Or was it a story Lucy invented?

Here is a passage from the novel that touches on something I have mentioned in this book—Frieda's will to save the artifacts of the past. The scene never really happened.

> First they took out the big dresser. They wrapped it in sheets and old blankets. They had to take it out the front door, then carry it around to the back of the house . . . They managed the move a few torturous steps at a time; Lucy didn't dare complain of the strain. They took their time arranging the boxes. It was a mournful job. Each box had to be opened and pawed through so that Greta could label it for stacking. She tucked folds of brown paper on top of the contents before closing and taping the flaps . . .
>
> They stood in the doorway of the little structure. It looked raw but sturdy. Before they put on the roof, the men had laid a thick layer of plastic. The biggest danger wouldn't be to the contents, but to anyone coming inside later, if they weren't cautious. This area was known for black widow spiders.
>
> . . . Greta had saved an old hand mirror of Laura's. It

wasn't even in perfect condition. But chipped or not, it had held her precious daughter's image.

Lucy was surprised to realize her eyes had filled with tears. She wiped them angrily. Greta closed the shed door and said, "I hope you're going to have a home of your own and come get all this. I'm saving it for you, you know that, don't you?" She snapped the padlock. "It's nothing to me, any of it. Everything's gone, for me."

Lucy's heart sank. She didn't want her mother's dishes. Every time she picked one up, her heart would break. And she didn't want to feed her grandmother's fantasy; some cruel impulse made her want to say it was junk, worth nothing; throw the damned stuff away! Instead, she nodded mutely, and then, seeing her grandmother's anguished expression, she embraced her for a long awkward moment. She should have said something. She should have said anything, but the rule was, swallow your words, chew on your sorrow. Opal had told Lucy many times: Mommy won't mix her grief with yours.

And what did it matter? Neither words nor storage would change the blackness of the holes in their world.

One Halloween Mae came with her kids. She had a sack of masks. She and Edith pulled together costumes for us. Frieda went out while we were dressing and climbed the little tree in front of her house. She was wearing a cape made out of a rag sheet. She waited there until our mothers herded us out for our circuit of trick-or-treating, and then she cried out, Whoo! Whoo! She tried to flap her cape, lost her footing, and fell off the branch and broke her ankle. It must have hurt terribly; they had to take her to the hospital, an expense she could ill afford, but all the way she was laughing. She wanted to know what the children thought. Was she too scary? Or just a little frightening?

A few years later, she took me to a wrestling match. She said someday I would look back and remember that I got to see Gorgeous George fight the Farmer and his pig. She bought good seats so we were close to the action. We didn't tell my mother.

ENIGMA

Frieda learned early not to rely on men. Even the good ones could suffer the vagaries of chance. First her farmer father died when a broken hame pierced his chest. Then, when she was thirty, her husband was blown off the back of a truck by a dust devil. She had three children and owned nothing. Hadn't Ira lent his Oklahoma highway department life insurance to his grasping father, never thinking what it was for? Didn't her father-in-law turn his back on her when she asked him when she might expect the money? And didn't that man and all his kin go about their comfortable lives while she lost her tiny house and took her children to live on her grudging stepfather's farm? While she left to work on the railroad for almost four years without her children?

She must have decided that every man to come after Ira better have something she needed. Joe helped her bring her children to Gallup in 1941, but while he was in the Army, she moved to Texas, divorced him, and never answered a letter to say what was on her mind. In 1953, Hamon came with a shell of a house. The two of them finished it and lived in it seven months before she filed for divorce. She paid him one dollar to assume the mortgage. And then there was Ben, her last companion. He sweet-talked her while he recovered from eye surgery in the nursing home where she worked; he was seventy years old, divorced, and lonely. She was sixty-seven. He only saw shadows, but he could sweet-talk. There's a girl under that belly fat, he said. He came with a travel trailer parked on a lot on a lake where the fishing was good. He liked to listen to football games on the radio while she watched them on TV, a habit she kept when he was long gone. It was true, what he said: she was getting old and fat around the middle. But she had mellowed, too. She didn't see the perfidy in him. Settled in the mild pleasures of companionship—someone to cook for, sounds in the house—she didn't see that he was flighty and childish. The marriage lasted not quite three years. One day he went back to his first wife to die, not that he had any reason to think death would happen soon. (It did.) He and Frieda had never quarreled. Maybe he was used to fighting and making up; something she had never tried.

I flew her out to Helena to visit me, my new husband, and my daughter, who was three years old. We were in Helena, Montana, and there was a lot for her to see there. She seemed tired. I was disappointed that she didn't pay much attention to my daughter, who might have cheered her up. She was polite, remote, as if she was trying to remember who we were.

Her divorce had been finalized just the week before she came. Are you okay? I asked after she had been there two weeks. We were standing in the doorway of the kitchen. She reached back and took a knife from the drain board. It glinted in the light that came through the kitchen window. She held it high in front of her chest.

She said, I dream I see him coming toward me in the street, and he can't see me. I have a knife, and I see myself driving it into his wattley throat. The sorry son of a bitch.

She let her arm drop. But I cross to the other side. What would be the point? Why kill a man? Let God take care of them. Let them burn in hell.

I like to think her outburst relieved her humiliation—for wasn't that it? That she had believed in a man, when she knew better?

A day later Sonny called to tell her that her sister, Frances, had gone into the hospital for exploratory surgery and had died on the operating table. Frieda flew home the next day. Whatever pain Ben had caused her was trivial and never mentioned again.

My aunt married early and got out of the house, but she was finished with that husband early on. She moved in with Frieda for a while, but then she married Howard, a tall drink of water who had an uncanny resemblance to Abraham Lincoln. I thought he hung the moon; all of us kids did. You'd have said: those two know how to have a good time.

But time wears a marriage down. That space in the middle of the bed gets wider. Kids grow up, move out, don't need you. What's left is worn out.

He took any long-drive job to be away from home. He ate greasy bacon and eggs every day even though she told him he was clogging his heart. He walked out on every quarrel. He poured his heart out to a woman in Hobbs. When Mae had had enough, Frieda helped her move to Lubbock to start over. She warned her, though: don't make the same mistake again. It wasn't like Frieda to speak straight out like that, but she had learned a lot the hard way, and she thought her daughter ought to have done so, too.

So when my aunt married a man who was ignorant and mean, Frieda only said, I'm leaving you my house, so you'll have some place to go when this is over.

When Frieda died, my aunt was still married, choking on it but not able to make a move. Besides, her crazy brother challenged the will, and everything was sold. She had had a pension from her years working for a physician, but her husband talked her into cashing out and investing in a sure thing that wasn't.

Oh Mae could have used Frieda's house soon enough, but by then it was gone. She found herself without a home or savings. She moved in with her daughter and grandson, who had only recently moved out from living with *her*. She got part-time work in a doctor's office. In that time, my cousin's little rented house swelled with more needy family. Eventually Mae got a settlement and could put a down payment on a house for all of them.

She took a job at Walmart in the fabrics department. At eighty-eight, she's still there. She says she needs the money, and it gets her out of the house.

met Allen Scofield when he came to Ithaca, New York, in May 1969 to visit a Navy buddy who lived in the same house as me. Years later, after our daughter was born and we had separated, an old graduate school friend came to visit me. Al came over for a few hours to work on the fence he was building for my house, and after he left, my friend said she was really surprised that I would marry "someone like that."

I burned with resentment at her remark, even though I know she didn't mean to hurt me. After all, I wasn't living with Al anymore, and she assumed I had had second thoughts, myself. I knew what she meant, too. He looked like a hippie. He dressed in old jeans and tee shirts. He had a moustache and longish hair. Shy, he hardly spoke around a stranger, even though she was a friend of mine. On top of that, he had enlisted in the Coast Guard and volunteered for a tour of Vietnam early in the war, and when I told her that, she was genuinely shocked. This was 1974, and vets were routinely vilified, as if they were responsible for the quagmire that was the war. In a bar on the Oregon coast, when Al was working for the railroad after he left the Coast Guard, he had been beaten by a couple of rednecks, not because they were opposed to the war, but because we were losing it. I had ended a friendship with another graduate school friend because when he learned I was pregnant with the child of a Vietnam veteran, he had smugly announced that *he* would have gone to Canada if he'd been drafted. *He'd* have gone to jail. (He was married with two children and never in the least danger of being drafted.)

Now this woman didn't like his looks. I didn't defend him; I didn't point out that he was college educated. I didn't say that I had fallen in love with him in an hour. I couldn't explain that there was a way of seeing the world and knowing that you lived outside the circle of people who matter and that meeting Al was like discovering kin in a landscape of aliens. I hadn't left him because he was different from me, but because he was exactly like me: a pessimist, an outsider, a melancholic. I left him because I had to be a part of the very world we had tried so hard to stay out of. I loved him, but I loved my daughter more, and I wanted her world to be a better place.

When my semester at Cornell University ended, Al and I had gone to Mexico for the summer. I already knew I wouldn't go back to complete my degree; I was on a new adventure. We took a drive-away car from Boston to El Paso, delivering it for a hockey player to his parents. Then we hitched to Laredo and took buses all the way to a small village on the Pacific coast, Zihuatenejo. Al had fallen in love with the place when his Coast Guard boat had stopped there, going from Florida to California.

Late in the summer I fell ill, and my aunt paid for a plane ticket for me to come to Monahans, Texas. Al followed on buses and hitched rides. I didn't know what my grandmother would think of him—or of us—but I knew that my aunt and uncle would welcome us.

They did better than that. Uncle Howard got Al a job driving for Halliburton for a month, replacing employees on vacation. We could save all of his salary, get an old car, and go on to California, where we had nothing in particular to do except find out what the fuss was all about.

Al had a moustache and a beautiful tangled mop of hair. His only clothes were jeans and ratty black tee shirts; he wore a uniform for his job. He loved the hot still air, the long empty highways, the big trucks. All those gears. When he was free he liked to drive out into the desert by himself and drink cold beer in the dark, then come back late, when everyone was asleep but me. We didn't have a car, but Mae hung her keys on a hook in the kitchen and said, mi caro, su caro. When he ate with the family, he tucked his head down shyly, though he always said it was good and he always said thank you. She liked his reticence and his appetite and the exoticism of having my Vietnam vet lover in her house. (We would marry in 1971.) We slept in different rooms—this was 1969 West Texas, after all. My uncle, a World War II Navy vet, respected Al's service and asked him about Vietnam, where Al had slid up threads of river to search fishermen's boats for weapons.

Then Frieda showed up in her little white Studebaker. The car was clunking, and we were all amazed she had made it from Wichita Falls. I introduced her to Al, and he stuck out his hand and said, keys. He pulled the car into the garage, scooted under, and went to work. Soon parts of Frieda's car were all over the garage floor. He spent two days under that car, stopping to go for parts, to eat, and hardly at all to sleep. I sat for hours at a time, leaning against the wall by the door into the kitchen listening to the radio, talking as if to myself, since he never answered. I don't remember what was wrong with the car, if I ever knew, but I know that it was serious and that it would have been costly to take it to a mechanic. Al cursed and banged tools, but he fixed the car. He didn't understand why anyone would drive a Studebaker. He took a long shower and reappeared to our applause. I made him a sandwich and towel-dried his hair. I wanted the others to see our intimacy; I was proud of him. I loved him.

You have to appreciate a man that handy, Frieda said. She tried to give him a twenty-dollar bill, but he wouldn't take it. I think that got to her as much as the repair work.

She got her keys, and we went to the store to get him a six-pack of beer. She said, buy something he really likes. Don't worry about what it costs.

When Al died in 1975, after he plowed his van into a parked car, coming too fast off a freeway exit, she told me, that boy loved you, and though it hurt a lot—I had left him by then, for just this reason, his recklessness, my fears—it was the right thing to say. Al and I had been in trouble more than once, some of it serious, and she had never suggested that I would be better off without him. She had never said that it—whatever it was at the time—was his fault. She admired him for his military service and for his practical skills, and she respected my feelings for him.

She did say to me once, though, the time she came to see my baby daughter, that it didn't use to take a man so long to grow up as it seemed to now.

And what difference does it make anyway? she might have said later. She might have thought. Her husband Ira grew up fast, worked hard, and died young; my Al saw a piece of the world and made me happy, some of the time, for a little while; then he died, too. So what good was grown-up love and responsibility in the end?

I know she was sorry about his death, as sorry as someone could be who loved me but was far away. It wasn't tragic, though, at least to her, because I didn't depend on him anymore. I had already left him, I had another husband. Not like when Ira died and she was thirty years old with three children.

I didn't think of Ira. I thought about my mother, because I thought her death was worse for me than Al's, but she had died a long time ago, and this was now. I could still remember the way he liked to sit on the floor, his arms resting on his knees, his head tucked, watching our baby learn to crawl.

The only person I could tell how much it hurt was my husband. I said it wasn't just Al; it was everybody. It was everything, so ephemeral. It was Al, and it was the "me" I wasn't anymore and maybe should never have been. I sat on the stairs that went down to the basement, and I cried, for hours, for months. I didn't cry that much again until Frieda died.

n 1953, my family was living with my widowed grandmother in a poor neighborhood of Wichita Falls, Texas. We were crowded, but it was what I had always known, and I was happy. Then she built a house on Grant Street, in the developing part of the city, much nearer the mill where she packed flour. I thought we would go with her; instead, we moved across the tracks past a Pig Stand Drive-In into county housing. Our duplex was not well furnished, but there my deeply religious mother, Edith, a Catholic convert, could set up an altar and hang devotional pictures. In Lutheran Frieda's house, Edith had said her prayers in a bedroom with the door closed. Her statue of the Blessed Virgin had sat on one wing of an old-fashioned dressing bureau, so that when she prayed, she faced both Mary and her own image in the large oval mirror.

I don't remember Frieda ever saying anything against Mother's Catholicism, and, in fact, for the last couple years before we moved, one of the priests had come to the house now and then to play Canasta, and Frieda had played, too. Once, I remember clearly, she and the priest had split a beer.

I know that Daddy was happy to move. He had always been a ghostly presence in Frieda's house. He sat on the back step until dark if the weather allowed, or he sat in the bedroom, reading paperback Westerns. He and Frieda never talked; if he came in from work—driving a cab or doing day labor on construction—he would say her name as he passed through a room. Frieda. With almost a question mark at the end. And she would give a quick nod without looking at him. If we were all together at the kitchen table, he ate with his head ducked down and excused himself to "see about" something. In our new apartment, of course, he could sit where he wanted, with his feet propped up on a rickety table; he played Solitaire and drank a beer after work. He clipped his toenails in the living room. He played the radio. We had more room, just the four of us in the two-bedroom apartment. I got used to being in our house and not my grandmother's, but I missed her. I hated the silverfish I sometimes saw crawling on my bedroom cinderblock wall, and I wished she could do something about it

We couldn't have moved with Frieda anyway, because she lived in the new house with a man, Collins Hamon. (She called him by his last name, in the manner of millworkers, policemen, and nurses.) They both worked at mills—she packed flour, he packed feed—and they had been friendly for a while, but none of us had ever met him. And though I now remember him vividly, because he behaved in a way I had never seen a man behave, the memory lay dormant for fifty years. Then, a long time after Frieda's death in 1983, I began reflecting on certain aspects of her life.

I was interested in learning about the Grant Street house because it was the house I had thought of as home base for nearly thirty years, and for most of that time, I had depended on my grandmother for her unconditional love. Facts are a scaffold for narrative, and though I didn't know it yet, I was searching for my grandmother's story. From public records, and much to my surprise, I learned that Collins Hamon bought the Grant Street property in 1949 for five thousand dollars and transferred ownership to Frieda in January 1953 for one dollar. (This is not to say that he gave her the house. Records also show that she paid the mortgage from 1953 to 1979.)

I always thought my grandmother had the house built—I had vivid memories of visiting the site with her—but what I saw must have been a nearly completed house on which she and Hamon did the finishing work. He had probably been living in it like a squatter; rough men need few amenities. As the house took final shape, it became her house. I was with her when she planted rose bushes in the front and two apricot trees near the back property line. This is my last house, she said. Her first house, in Chickasha, Oklahoma, had been emptied by her husband's death twenty years earlier.

My mother didn't let me visit Frieda through the summer months, but in the fall she relented. I went to Grant Street on Saturdays and was home again by dark. Frieda had a television set (we did not), women's magazines, and paper for my drawings. Sometimes we drove to my great-grandparents' farm in Devol, Oklahoma, for a few hours. Other times we did small chores, like the laundry. I folded clothes while I told Frieda about school. Were Hamon's clothes there? I don't think so. I don't think I would forget something so odd, so thrillingly repulsive. I thought he was ugly and strange, but I knew my grandmother would never leave me alone with him for even a moment.

He went in and out of the house a lot, banging doors. He muttered and cursed. Although I didn't think Frieda liked him, and I didn't understand why he was there, it never occurred to me to ask. I didn't know they were married, nor did I wonder about it. Adults did what they did, and children fit in around them. I would never have talked about him to my mother, because I thought if she knew how rough he was, she would say I couldn't go to the house.

Frieda had been widowed since 1936 and was still a young woman, but I think in time she became ashamed of the choice she had made, and her shame turned to bitterness, as grief had done before. Now my writer's mind runs freely over their history: meetings with friends from the mills, the flattery of his attention, maybe his look that suggested things she want-ed—not vulgar things, but intimacies, a try at not being alone. And there was the property.

Now and then Hamon's daughter, C., was at the house when I was. She was twelve years old, a polite and pleasant girl who lived with her dead mother's parents. We were too old to play, and we had nothing to talk about. Usually she studied or read.

She kept her head down. Soon I learned why.

Hamon beat her. I remember the first time I was there when it hap-pened. I was at the kitchen table. I heard his harsh voice, her yelps, and then he stormed through the kitchen pushing her ahead of him toward outside as she whimpered that she was sorry, so sorry. I looked through the window, and I saw that he had taken her to the far end of the large back lot, by the alley near my grandmother's apricot trees. He swung his arm around and hurled it hard against her back and she twisted away, then tumbled to the ground.

I didn't think he would hit me, but he was a frightening, monstrous man, and I rushed to find my grandmother. She was in the spare bedroom changing the sheets.

Did you forget I was here? Why didn't you come get me? I cried.

I also asked, What did she do so bad? Why is he hurting her? Aren't you going to do anything?

Frieda pulled me into the bedroom and shut the door. She stood behind me and put her arms around me until my breathing was regular again. She was a hard-muscled, skinny woman, who lifted fifty-pound bags of flour every day.

She turned me around to face her: It's none of our business. You hear?

That was her way of saying I shouldn't talk or worry about it. (A father beats his child.) She would always protect me. But it was not up to her to protect C.

I never said anything to my mother about these incidents. I added C. to my prayers at daily Mass before school.

Once C. screamed at her father, I hate you! She ran, if you can call it that, but Hamon, snorting with menace, was always between her and an exit door. She darted about the house while he feinted and grabbed at her and finally, inevitably, caught her blouse at the back. She wrenched away, and I heard the ripping of the blouse as he tore it off her body. My grandmother and I stood in the doorway of her bedroom like people waiting out a tornado.

When my grandmother planted her trees, I imagined myself checking the apricots on them, watching for the warm colors as they ripened. I imagined myself carrying them in my apron to the kitchen. But I don't think I ever went near the trees. Frieda made wonderful fried pies stuffed fat with stewed fruit, and I liked them and ate them, but I think I could do this only because the golden crusts and the oozing apricots were so far removed in time and form from the trees and the girl with her father.

Hamon never hit C. in the face, but her arms bore bruises the color of eggplant. I saw him pull his arm back with savage deliberation and swing hard against her body. Once this happened in the house, and she thudded against a doorjamb and her eye swelled shut. My grandmother drove her home, then me. Hamon left the house a few weeks later, and he and Frieda divorced soon after. It was as if he had never existed.

C.'s maternal grandparents were able to go to court to stop her father from seeing her again. She disappeared from my grandmother's house and from my life.

In the 1964–65 school year, I lived with my grandmother and taught at the Catholic school where I had once been a student. One Sunday we saw in the newspaper that C. had married a doctor. Frieda said she was very happy for her. Hamon had long ago left Wichita Falls, had probably killed himself drunk in a car by now, she said. (In fact, he died many years later in California.)

When I was much older than Frieda had been that year, I wondered why she would marry someone she did not love and overlook his brutality toward his child. I told myself that it was something about the times, when many parents kicked their children or beat them with belts and fists and sticks and almost no one interfered, not kin nor neighbor, church brethren, or the law. There had been a girl in her old neighborhood who was never allowed off her porch except for school or church. I had often heard the boy across the street yelping as his father struck him across the back of his legs. I'm sure my grandmother believed she had no right to interfere. I have considered that she might have been afraid of Hamon. These explanations have not put my mind at ease. She was a woman who much loved children, and yet it seemed she had cared nothing about C.

I didn't think until recently that Hamon was a man with strong arms and that the house he helped Frieda finish would be her home until her death, or that she might not have been able to buy the house on her own. I didn't think until now about the times my uncle lived in her house, the times that I did, or the two years after my mother died when she rented that house so that she could live with me in Odessa until I finished high school.

All the times she would have said: Thank God I have my house.

I didn't think until recently that from the beginning she might have meant to use Hamon and that it might have surprised her to see how much it cost her to do so. Once she was young and happy, and then she lost her happiness, and where there had once been joy and faith and hope, anger and pragmatism took cold hold.

Frieda is one of legion: women who have stood at graves and at the doors of empty houses and seen a sea of empty prospects. I don't know if she made a conscious decision to ignore her husband's abuse or if she turned her face out of helplessness. I don't know if she had seen violence and knew its name or if she cared so much for so many that she had no room in her heart for another mother's child. It isn't my place to judge my grandmother, to forgive her, or to try to balance that strange year against her suffering and her good acts. She failed that girl. But I believe that as we must seek the right path and do the right things, we must also look inside ourselves for all the ways we are not what we should be, or even who we think we are. I am a writer because I believe there is a kind of word that takes us into the human heart and lays it bare, and I think it is a life's work to find a way to speak it.

ANGER

Eph. 26-27: Be angry but do not sin; do not let the sun set on your anger, and do not leave room for the devil.

I didn't really want to teach high school, but when Al and I moved to Berkeley, California, in October 1969, and I learned that a beginning teacher made ten thousand dollars a year, I started looking. There was a large high school in Fremont where an English teacher had left his position unexpectedly, and when the principal learned that I could teach English, speech, and drama, he sent me to the district office to sign a contract.

It was a terrible time to be there. Fremont was a blue-collar town where factory workers made high wages. Their kids had a lot of spending money, cars, motorcycles. And drugs. The favorite drugs were downers, because you could float through a boring school day. Teachers had a protocol to follow. If a student laid his head on his desk and didn't raise it when his name was called twice, the teacher rang the office, and the student was removed by security guards. I felt awkward and alien in my classes, but I directed two plays and enjoyed working with the cast and crew. By Christmas I was able to replace the junk car we had driven from Texas, and I felt safer making my commute. I was relieved to have a decent salary. There were two teachers I liked. Two.

The principal was a retired naval commander, and he loved to talk about keeping a tight ship. He hated the teachers' union. I never understood what the issues were, but there was always a lot of agitation in the building, undercurrents of resentment toward the administration. The principal asked me several times when was I going to buy nicer clothes. When a memorandum came around in the early spring asking teachers to state their intentions for the coming year, I was so desperate to escape, I checked "Retire." The principal called me in just to laugh about it.

I found an open position north of San Francisco in Napa County. The town was small and scenic, with large vineyards and elegant estates. The school district offered me a job. I would direct a play in the spring, coach debate, teach one general speech course, and the rest of my schedule would be basic English classes with the children of Mexican immigrant workers. Those families lived in shabby housing that had been built by the vintners to support a stable work force. I was happy to make the move. Al and I headed off to Oregon for the summer, camping along the coast and then in the eastern part of the state. When we came back, I rented a small house behind its owner's large one, on a huge lot that had another house nearby, rented to a young couple. My landlord asked me to please keep the noise down and to water the lawn every other day; everything was parched tinder, and there was a danger of fire until the winter rains. I promised I would water, rake the yard, be careful, and be quiet.

Then I put up my posters of Bob Dylan and Woody Guthrie, bought some groceries, and put sheets on a mattress on the floor. I had a radio, and we could get San Francisco stations. Both of us loved blues and rock. We bought a small table and two chairs at a thrift store in nearby Napa and called it home. I wrote my grandmother to tell her I was going to make eleven thousand dollars as a teacher, and I promised to come see her at Christmas.

We must have been crazy. Al and I weren't married, and though he was a skilled carpenter and mechanic, there was nothing for him to do in the town. We had been living in Berkeley, where nobody cared what you looked like or how you lived. Napa Valley was wholly conservative. I didn't notice. Miss Oblivious, that was me. I liked the new school and threw myself into my classes. English as a Second Language wasn't a public school discipline yet, and I had to make things up as I went along. The kids were shy with me, but they needed so much that whatever I did was good enough. Also, they didn't intimidate me the way the Bay Area students had. I met some of their parents and learned that they were trying to get support to build better housing that they would own. I offered to write or rewrite their grant proposals and to go over permit regulations with them. Then a judge in Marin country was murdered in his courtroom, and the Black activist Angela Davis was accused of participating in the plans. She became a fugitive. Where I was living, you could feel the anger and fear gathering like storm clouds. The little local newspaper was full of letters about hippies and radicals and the decline of respect and American decency.

Disgusted, Al took off for Oregon for a while. And I? I was young and full of confident conscience. I was dumb as a post. I wrote a high-minded letter to the editor expressing my outrage that people were deciding guilt and potential punishment (the death penalty, of course) before anybody had been tried. The editor called me and invited me to come and talk to him. He served me iced tea. He said he wasn't going to publish my letter, even though he agreed with my principles; it would bring me enormous grief. He tried to make me understand the position I was in as a teacher. He was kind and wise, and I was offended.

In the faculty lounge, I talked about politics and freedom. I complained about being censored. I typed documents for the Mexicans.

The superintendent called me in. What he had to say was much like the newspaper editor's talk with me, only now my job was on the line. The superintendent was cold, firm, scrupulously courteous. I protested, then sulked, but I understood, at last, where I was. He didn't want to ruin my career or create a crisis at the school, he said, but he thought I was not right for the district. I promised to teach, refrain from all my "Mexican politicking," and we agreed that I would leave my contract at the end of the first semester with a positive reference. That gave me time to look for something else. The administrator also mentioned that I wasn't doing myself any favor living in an illicit relationship. I informed him that my "friend" wasn't even in town, and when he was, we would be discreet. (In fact, we had never been to a public place together. There wasn't anything to do in town; we never even went to a café.)

Al reappeared, heard about my tribulation, and laughed. He had a guiding principle: Keep your head down. We'll ride it out, he said. Then we'll go to Portland.

He decided he would build a dory—a small flat-bottomed fishing boat—for something to do. There was an attached garage where he could work. He had built a dory earlier in the year in Sausalito, working on the deck of a small houseboat he had rented. He had sold it for a nice sum, and he was sure he could sell another one in the same area. I behaved myself at school, avoiding interaction with anyone other than my students. At night, while I wrote plans or read, Al drank beer and smoked the last of his stash of marijuana. He took some seeds from the bottom of the baggie and planted a few at the back of the house where no one would see the plants. I didn't know what he had done. I wasn't interested in drugs or drinking, but I wasn't in charge of Al. I knew he would do what he wanted, whatever I thought, and I didn't care. I just wanted him to be there when I came home after school. I wanted him to love me.

We had a fire. It wasn't because I didn't water the weeds, though I didn't. Faulty wiring in the garage caused a spark that ignited a pan of oil Al had just drained from his van. The firemen arrived quickly. The garage was gone in minutes, but they saved the house. The dory, set up on sawhorses on the gravel drive, was untouched.

Our young neighbors invited us to their home to shower and have supper. I couldn't eat; in fact, I threw up and could only sip water. Our hostess said the fire was bound to be upsetting, but I thought I had the flu. I had been nauseated all week. She said she would make up a bed for us. Al and I wanted to check on the house, to see the damage. We said we would be right back.

The firemen had left hours earlier, but a squad car and two policemen were waiting for us. It was Al's spindly baby marijuana plant at the back of the house that brought havoc into my life. The firemen had just had special training to look for signs of drug use. They must have been very proud of themselves.

The district attorney heaped charges on us, absurd ones like contributing to the delinquency of minors (none had ever been in the house) and intent to distribute. Al had some firecrackers in his van and the D. A. called them "explosives." The last few tablets of medicine for my intestinal illness in Mexico two summers earlier mysteriously moved from the prescription bottle to a baggie and were described as "illicit narcotics."

I was released on my own recognizance. I bailed Al out with money I borrowed from the religious Sisters in Fort Worth who had been my teachers in high school. They wired it to me within hours of my desperate call.

A teacher from the Fremont school took us in. I didn't have the flu; I was pregnant. I couldn't sleep, and I was sick all the time, but I worked Kelly Girl jobs to stay busy and accrue money for legal fees. I found a lawyer in San Francisco who was originally from Napa; he seemed amused at the idea of taking on the county and agreed to accept as fee whatever we could scrape together. I sold my car and camera. The lawyer took all my money and Al's dory and had me come into his office to work as a file clerk. After a couple of months and one court appearance, he told us that nobody really cared about us; they just wanted us out of their hair. I took that as advice. I called my grandmother, Frieda, who lived in Texas, and told her I was going to go to Canada for a while. I talked in riddles and cried. She must have been frightened for me, and I'm sure she didn't understand what we had done or why it couldn't be put right, but she didn't say. She would have done anything to help. I had known she couldn't have come up with the money I had needed for Al's bail, but now I asked her for a few hundred dollars to make her know I needed her. We took a bus to British Columbia. Before we left I wrote her: Please don't be mad at me.

I had seen my grandmother's anger all my life, but I had never been afraid of it, because I knew it was about the world and not about me. It was manifested in pursed lips and swollen silence; it infested the family and made us suspicious and wary of outsiders. She knew things, but she didn't speak of them, and we were always trying to guess what had happened, what had been done. After she died, my aunt and I tried for years to talk about her anger, but we missed her, and we couldn't remember or didn't like to remember too much. It seemed disloyal to remember her anger because, really, we remembered it as a fault, and we wanted better memories of her. We wanted her to have had a better life.

I had observed, in my childish way, that Frieda resented rich people and most men. Widowed young, she hated that fate had cheated her of happiness. Her oldest child, my mother, had died at thirty-three after long suffering. Frieda had had a life full of pain and grief and unfairness, and she had minded mightily, but she had never run away or called attention to herself. She had banked her anger, drawing on it, I sometimes think, to fire her strength: for working overtime; for bailing out her children from ill health and fiscal woes; for the husbands that came and went like bad weather; for nursing her mother in her last days; and her stepfather, too, whom she did not love, in his. She was never angry with us grandchildren. We all adored her. I could not have named the concept of unconditional love until I was a schooled adult, but I basked in it all my childhood.

In Canada, on the Sechelt Peninsula, Al and I found a rough shed on a hillside where the owner was clearing land for an RV park, and we lived there, and Al worked for him while I spent my days worrying about the baby and walking up and down the road in the cold rain. I heard from some hippies about a phone that you could use to call the U.S. and it returned your coins. It was true! It was weeks before the phone company sent someone all the way out to our tiny outpost to fix it. I called my grandmother to tell her I was pregnant and then three or four more times to say I was okay, trying not to cry. She mailed me a warm coat and rain boots. She said I should see a doctor for the baby soon. I promised her I would, and I did, in a crazy scheme with a fraudulent medical card. It was just the one time, and I was pronounced healthy, maybe a little underweight, and I was urged to drink milk and eat chicken and fresh fruit. I spent most of my time in bed reading books from the tiny library in the village two miles away. I ate eggs and sweet brown cheese and salami, crackers, and chocolate bars.

In a while I got large with the baby, and I wanted to go back to the U.S. I wanted to go to Texas, but it was too far away. I thought I would go there after the baby was born. Frieda would love my baby. Al probably wouldn't go with me. I was already moving away from him, toward the child.

A friend of Al's came up in his truck to Canada and got us, and other generous friends in Portland, Oregon, took us in. I saw a doctor, who scolded me for not taking vitamins. That wasn't the problem, though. The problem was that I couldn't start labor on my own. I kept telling them, it's time, it's late, I'm huge, something is wrong; but I was poor, so obviously I was ignorant, too. Al's friend, a social worker, told me how to get admitted to the hospital: stand at the entrance to ER and scream, It's coming! It's coming! and don't stop. That worked. They induced labor, but it took twenty-six hours for them to notice it wasn't going very well. There was a Mexican woman in the labor room who had been brought from the county jail. Her legs were shackled to the bed, and I was glad I had run away, though I wanted to stop being scared and ashamed.

The baby was too big to deliver, but it was too late for a C-section. Now they would have to make cuts, break bones. They put me in an operating room with a large viewers' gallery. By then I was floating on a morphine dream. I knew something bad was happening, but I wasn't strong enough to catch on to what it was. I was in a teaching hospital. A dozen students filed in to watch. I wondered if they were there because we were something special, like a puzzle or a car wreck. I forgot about them after a few minutes, although much later I saw them in my mind so clearly, wearing white coats and leaning toward one another to whisper.

The doctors spoke to me. The baby's shoulders—they couldn't have known. A social worker came to make sure I knew about birth control.

They said they would take care of Baby; they would keep him comfortable. He wasn't able to suck, and they would not feed him another way. He was a bruiser, he didn't look damaged at all. He was a big beautiful boy. He deserved to live, but I thought it was all my fault that he didn't. Now I know that nobody paid any attention to me for twenty-six hours, because I was poor and I didn't know what to demand. A resident had come on duty and said, angrily, Doesn't anybody know anything? To me, he was gentle. He said, It's very late, Sandra. You must be brave.

Sign this, someone said, and I did, and then the hospital took care of everything. Someone came with a form, and I named him Jake. There was no funeral.

I was never able to tell anyone what happened. I said, my baby died, and before long I didn't mention him anymore. Nobody would want to hear about the pain, the confusion, and dread, the feeling of being a specimen, an experiment, instead of a person. The humiliation. My anger that they hadn't listened to me. And the shame of having let the baby go like I did. Of course Frieda was a nurse and my grandmother; she would have listened to my story, I'm sure. She would have been angry, too. But she was in Texas, and on the phone, I could barely speak.

By the time I was pregnant with my daughter, I had a good job and was part of the Kaiser medical system. The first doctor I saw was the resident who had appeared too late to save my boy. He said every doctor in the clinic would understand my history, he would see to it. There was ultrasound now. We would set a due date and stick to it. It turned out to be easy, birthing my daughter. I went into the hospital on New Year's Eve, our due date. My water broke, but they had to induce labor. I thought: I am forgiven.

In the fall we went to California. We had borrowed money from the father of Al's friend the social worker, and a lawyer from Sausalito represented us.

He said they were mad at us, so they would surely give Al a short county sentence, but they would take one look at me and send me home. I was haggard and crying constantly. I had been through a lot. And I truly had not known about the plants.

We both went to county jail for three months, though two weeks were suspended, and we were released on Christmas Eve.

The other women were hard on me. I was very thin and jumpy. There were whores, drunk drivers, check kiters, shoplifters, and a woman whose baby had died a crib death for which she was blamed. SIDS was a new, still suspicious, concept.

The jail was new and clean; everything was made of concrete and steel. There was nothing for us to do. I cried because my lips were grievously chapped. We wore flip-flops and Sears housedresses; my feet were cold and achy. The only available reading was three books of condensed novels; I read them over and over. Women stole my candy bars and came to my bunk after lights-out to punch me, but I didn't yell or tattle or care.

Then the women learned from one of the matrons that my baby had died soon after he was born, and they let up, though they sat away from me on the bolted steel stools where we sat and watched TV in the late afternoons. Nobody ever spoke to me, and after lights-out, I cried with my face in my pillow.

A woman in the community heard about me, and she brought a huge sack of yarn and crochet needles to the jail. You wouldn't have thought they would let the needles in, but she was the wife of someone important, and it was almost Christmas by then. Besides, none of us were violent offenders. One of the prisoners, a Latina in her mid-twenties, a new mother herself, knew how to make crocheted squares and was a willing teacher. In the afternoons, four or five of us sat up on a big stainless steel ledge in the day room crocheting while the matron watched us, drinking coffee and chatting in a friendly way. Something about the crocheting made everyone relax and tell stories, and at night I repeated the stories to myself until I fell asleep, wanting to remember them because I had never heard anything like them and because it helped if I thought of the women as characters in their interesting lives and not as people who had hurt me. The black woman who had hit me the hardest said she had always wanted to know how to make something with her hands.

I made a small afghan for my grandmother out of stiff, ugly orange and yellow and brown acrylic yarns. I mailed it to her as soon as I was released. After she died in 1983, it came to me in her things, wrapped around a statue of the Blessed Virgin that had been my mother's. A few years ago I threw it away because it was ugly, but I still think of the time I visited my grandmother in her house and saw it folded neatly on her closet shelf. It prompted me to tell her how sorry I was about "all that." By then I had had my daughter, and I was in many ways like a person in recovery, shuffling through my history, making amends.

She had never asked for any of the details, and I didn't give them, though I would have liked to tell someone about the women in the jail and about the food and the boredom. I should have told her about the baby. Every day after I was released from the hospital, I took three buses to get to the hospital and sit with him, until the day he died. But now I had a beautiful daughter, and I wanted Frieda to think I was happy.

I said it had been a trivial matter but a big misunderstanding at a time when people were scared of youth and hair and color and anyone's opinions unlike their own. Al and I had made a mistake, living in a conservative little town where we never should have been; people had mixed us up with other people we would never be.

That was when she told me that two FBI men had come to her house looking for me. I don't know what shocked me more, that anyone could have thought I was a person of consequence or that she could have kept their visit to herself. I was flooded with embarrassment and indignation. My experience with the legal system had fed my resentment of authority. At the same time, I realized instantly that Frieda hadn't fully understood or cared that I had been responsible for what had happened to me: I had broken the law, in however minor a way, and however exaggerated and unfair the accusations were, I had brought them on myself. Indeed, I had not yet absorbed or admitted this; I had not examined the experience, only lived it, then scrambled to start my life again, struggling to shed my fears, trying to sort out a way to start fresh like the adult I had to be in order to raise my child. At least I had a good job, the kind that lets you have time off to take your new baby home to Texas. Al and I had married after our baby died, though our relationship was mortally wounded by our experience with crime and punishment. He wanted to pick up where he left off, living his ambling life; I wanted everything tidy and safe and respectable. I didn't think better of society's rules, but now I feared them.

I wanted to tell Frieda that things would get better soon, that I would be more and more like other people, but she spoke first. She said, They asked to come into my house, and I said, Do I have to do that? Is there a law that says I have to let you in without a warrant? And you know there is not. I stood in the doorway. They were uncomfortable on my step. They had come out here and they must have known there was nothing for them, they must have known we were no threat.

I heard that "we," as if she were complicit in my misdemeanors.

She glowed with anger. I was in awe of her audacity. All along I had seethed with indignation: Why couldn't they see my innocence! (Or at least my innocuousness.) But I had whimpered and held my tongue, while she had stood up to the FBI, whom she saw as invaders and false accusers of her family. Her outrage was fresh as she remembered the men at her door.

It was the first time I realized that her anger, always present, visible as a night-light, could be called up and focused; that it held within it the potential for havoc. She felt justified in her wrath because the men had had it so wrong, and she had learned the Psalms as a child: ". . . thou has broken the teeth of the ungodly" (Psa 3:3). Maybe those men had not pushed her far enough, but someone could. Even as I was glad to have her love me, I was repulsed by her zeal.

I hadn't learned the beautiful power of anger when it is rooted in God's love. I had not associated it with Jesus in the temple, casting out the moneychangers. I had never seen it on the faces of strong people standing up to injustice and suffering, because I had never looked, although there had been civil rights marches in the South while I was having dubious adventures and wondering if anything in life would ever have meaning.

Something stirred: a sorrow for the many times I had hurt her with my absences and my waste of opportunities and her steady love. I ached for her to care about something better, steadier and more deserving than me, something worthy of her defiance. Something holy.

And even more I wanted the sweetness I knew in her to be reflected in what she saw around her. Oh, I would be that sweetness! I thought, I with my child. I would never again give her reason to worry about me. I would give her reason to shed her anger and love the world.

I wouldn't have believed it if someone had told me that in a few short years she would suddenly grow old and look inward where I could see nothing, where I had no place and from where she barely bothered to hold me in her weary vision. I wish I had known: I wish I had thought to look to that common ground we must have had in our different faiths and to step into it with her right then, to seek joy and the surcease of bitterness. I like to think this is what she was doing in the last months of her life when she was so much alone with her photographs, her Bible, her cache of clipped poems from half-century-old newspapers, but she never gave us a hint.

We knew her anger all our lives, but when she let it go in her dying, she had told us nothing of what filled her in its place. She made it clear that it was none of our business. My aunt said Frieda wasn't getting enough blood to her brain, and I shouldn't take anything personally. But when my grandmother turned away from me that last summer, I thought it was my fault, perhaps a punishment, and I can't shake the sadness of losing her before she died.

The hard lines of her face did soften a little that day, and I thought that I had breached the space between us and closed the sorry narrative of my bad behavior, but no, there was one more thing she had to say.

They stepped down lightly and didn't look the least surprised. They didn't even seem to mind. I said to the one who was closest to me, Young man, I don't know what else you have to worry about, but there must be more important things than my granddaughter. She's a good girl, and she's never hurt anyone but herself.

And then you called me that very night on your peculiar free phone, and I said, don't you worry, sugar, you'll be all right in spite of everything.

And I am.

In 1975 the Napa County court expunged my record, but not Al's. It didn't matter, because he was dead.

F rieda was a frugal woman, a saver of string. She kept a big sugar bowl on the stove filled with bacon grease. She scooped it out to fry potatoes or okra or to season beans. Whatever food was left over at the end of a meal went into cups covered by pieces of waxed paper and secured with rubber bands. She never threw away a sheet, a washcloth, a cooking pot, a worn-out blouse. Thin linens folded neatly; eventually everything was thin. Worn clothes became rags or quilt scraps. Her house bulged with items saved for future use, too good to be thrown away. When she died, there were still feed sacks from her parents' farm folded in the hall cupboard with the towels. The refrigerator that had been in my mother's house when she died in 1959 was still in use in Frieda's kitchen when she died in 1983. There was an element of economy, of course, but I never opened the door without thinking: this was my mother's refrigerator.

Frieda kept Mother's wing-backed chair, upholstered in gold damask, in her bedroom where no one would sit in it. When I lived with her I brought home bundles from the laundromat (we called it the "washateria") and threw them on her bed, then piled the folded clothes on the chair. There was always a moment when I simply gazed at it, burdened for a long moment with my mother's loss. The chair was full of story: how Mother had worked as a waitress to buy it on layaway; how she had put away other things—lamps, a watch, dresses—and lost them for nonpayment; how I sat in the chair at the foot of her bed when she was dying. Frieda would never have sold it to strangers, or worse, let Daddy take it.

I had lived with Frieda after Mother died in 1959, although not in this house. I was in high school in Odessa, and Frieda rented a little house for us and took leave from the flour mill. She entered training at Odessa Junior College to become a licensed vocational nurse. It was a rigorous program; she studied for two years while working part time at the hospital. We moved everything that had belonged to Mother with us, and when Frieda went back to Wichita Falls, she took those things with her. Mother's clothes were crammed into garment bags and stuffed into the hall closet against the water heater. Her silverware, black with tarnish and wrapped in bags with velvet ties, was stored in a wooden chest under the bed. There was all the Catholic paraphernalia: crucifixes, rosaries, statues, prayer books. Her pretty white dishes with the green trim. Boxes of clippings, papers, photographs. Frieda fit what she could under the bed and between the bed and the wall, then built a storage shed in the backyard to hold the overflow.

Later, when her mother died and her stepfather went to live with his own daughter, Frieda crammed in furniture from the farm, packing the house so tight you could not walk without brushing something with your hip. She held it all for her grandchildren, but, sadly, she had no takers. She said we would want these things later; we would realize their worth. I always thought she had rejected the past because it was unsalvageable, but now I think she wanted me to remember: my mother, her mother, herself. *Things* encapsulated her unspoken memories and respect.

Her patience was stoic but accusing. As soon as I married, she called to ask if I would come to collect my mother's things. She would throw in her parents' car for good measure. I stalled. She did not understand how tenuous was my connection to the marriage, work, property, propriety. She did not live long enough to see how profoundly I would change, though I am sure that she was happy to see me "settled." I spent my young adulthood free-floating, moving on an hour's notice, a bitter source of anguish for her, yet never receiving her reprimand. I left belongings in my wake like a refugee, coast to coast and as far south as Huatulco.

I had no room for Mother's marble-top end table or cross-stitched towels faded at the folds. I believed that things perish and are best abandoned early. I had no energy for the past and not a hint of understanding of how much more of the past was held not in my grandmother's house, but in her psyche. She had lost her father as a child, the father of her own children when they were little, a daughter who was only thirty-three. Somehow, all that had passed to me, and I took it as a mantra: lose now or lose later. When my first baby died twelve days after his birth, I let the hospital take the body; I simply could not manage. I couldn't begin to think of a funeral, a grave. For me, for so long, loss had no corollary of memory and steward-ship. It was something to run from. It was unfair, something done to me. Now I dream of graves, a field of everyone I loved; the baby, too. And me.

When Frieda died, she left her house neatly sorted. She must have spent the whole summer arranging and labeling. I try to believe that she was comforted by a conviction that in her death she would finally get her wish: that we grandchildren would take into our homes the artifacts she had saved for us, and we would free them from their boxes and restore them to utility and honor them for their connection to those who had loved us so much.

Perhaps she imagined all of us parked every which way on the dead grass, taking things away in little trailers or tied on the roofs of our cars. She could not have guessed that everything would be sold from her front yard, forced into auction by her son's mad challenge to the will. She would not have dreamed that her treasures would go home to strangers. Her mother's table! Her daughter's bed!

I wish I had gone to her in those months before she died, but some-times I think that at the end—by then she wanted so much for it to be over—she opened wide to oblivion, finally free from my mother, not really believing she would join her in heaven, but trusting that there would be peace at last; falling past everything, finding nirvana the way holy people do, in surrender.

What I know about my grandmother comes in these ways: from the memory of her behavior, which sheltered and cosseted me, but also per-plexed me at times; from the artifacts that came to me when she died, in the few boxes we were allowed from the house by the court-appointed executor; from my amateur research into the places where she lived; and from the memories of my Aunt Mae.

I wish I had learned more from Frieda herself. When she told stories, they often turned out to be anecdotes about my own childhood, stories I had already heard, stories meant to remind me that I had once been the center of a universe. I wonder now if she thought no one would be interested in her life. She told me once that from her stepfather's farm she had to walk two miles to school on country roads and that in the winter she carried a hot potato in each pocket as hand warmers and then ate them at lunch. I thought this was a quaint *Little House on the Prairie* story, but when I think about it now, I remember the other part: how when her little half-sister went to school, someone drove her there in a car with a heater. The potatoes were only a tiny part of the real story, which had to do with Frieda's loss of her father and her uneasy place in the new family her mother's second marriage made. (And only now do I realize that her experience must have prejudiced her against my stepfather—the very idea of a stepfather. She didn't just love me. Whether she knew it or not, she loved the child she once was.)

She told me that she played basketball in high school, on a team that went all the way to state, but she didn't tell me about the young woman who went off to Chickasha to business college and met Ira Hambleton. Nothing of that skinny young bride, besotted with love. When, a few years after she died, I held in my hand a photograph of the two of them, he so handsome, she so tenderly embraced, I burst into tears. I simply could not believe the joy on their faces. I had never heard her speak his name. (The few times she spoke of him, she called him "the children's Papa.")

I had not known that she had once been happy.

When I opened the boxes that came to me after her death, I was struck by how undisturbed things were. I wondered at her sense of privacy; I still had things to learn about her allegiance to sworn secrets. I realized that the meaning of the documents and artifacts did not lie in their words and images but in their survival, that they existed at all. To her, they were relics. The past, worn thin like the towels in her hall cupboard, could be handed down. The next person could look and parse the meaning of it all, because she had taken care. She had to have known I would be the one, if anyone, to appreciate the gift. I wish she could know how grateful I am.

She was about thirty-five when she developed mouth cancer. She had been working for the railroad, traveling with crews in New Mexico and Arizona, living and cooking for the men in a boxcar. She had finally been able to move to Gallup, New Mexico, and had brought her children to join her.

She had to take the bus to Albuquerque, hours away from Gallup, for treatment. My aunt says she doesn't know how Frieda paid for it. They were poor. The kids took care of themselves—the girls were teenagers, and Sonny was a little boy who did what he wanted to do anyway.

The doctors excised the tumor and put her through a series of torturous irradiation treatments; bits of radium were implanted in the roof of her mouth. She went through the treatments as an outpatient, staying overnight in a shabby rented room nearby, walking back and forth to the hospital. Then she took the bus back to Gallup until the next round of treatments. Once home, she went back to work.

I try to imagine how it happened. There would have been a small nodule on the roof of her mouth, or perhaps an ulcer. There probably wasn't pain when she first noticed it. She worried it with her tongue, wondering if it would go away, but absorbing its presence so that it became ordinary. Then something changed, and the pain came, maybe not where the tumor was, maybe in her throat or her ear, or maybe if the surface was ulcerated, bits of skin came off on her tongue. She had trouble eating. She couldn't just be brave and bear it; if she died, her children would be orphaned. Maybe she borrowed the money from her employer. All her life she would borrow small sums and pay them back, in cycles of near despair.

She was very thin, but wiry and tough. Through the time of the surgery and radiation treatments, she could hardly swallow nourishment, even liquids, and she grew gaunt. One by one, her teeth loosened. Soon she would have them all pulled.

Between treatments, she lay on the rented bed, staring at the ceiling, worrying about her children. What would become of them if she did not recover? They had been a family living in Chickasha, Oklahoma, when Ira Hambleton died, and there had been households of his kin—preachers, teachers, and businessmen—but nobody helped her. She lost her house and took work with the railroad, depositing her children on her stepfather's farm. She knew that Mae would never go back there again.

She lay on her rented bed, her lips drawn in, her gums swollen and sore, and I think she struck a kind of bargain with God. She knew she was going a little far—Lutherans didn't do this sort of thing—but she thought maybe she had earned a bit of mercy. If she lived, she would take care of her children, and then she would take care of their children, if she needed to do so; she would live as if her doors did not latch; she would save nothing for herself if her kin needed a single thing. All she asked was to go on.

Was that when she swore the promises that governed her life as I saw it while growing up?

I will never complain. I will never ask, why me?

I will never speak ill of the dead.

I will never dwell on the unfairness of calamity.

I will work while there is breath in me.

I will take care of everyone I love.

I will stand against all outsiders who would hurt any of them.

I will not lament.

Would she have made such a contract, and thus recover? The cancer never recurred, though she lost her teeth. She did not complain.

Her expression said this: My lips are sealed.

Her furious, furious silence ruled us all. Her anger infected everyone, but her love was absolute.

LEGACY

FRIEDA'S LARDER

Milk, buttermilk, butter, eggs
White bread (home baked)
Cornbread
Saltine crackers; graham crackers
Buttermilk biscuits
Oatmeal
Cheerios, Grape Nuts
Bacon; ham hocks
Bacon grease (for frying potatoes, for gravy)
Chicken (fried; stewed with dumplings)
Pork chops, salt pork
Ground beef (cheap in Texas)
Ham (rarely)
Potatoes, mashed or fried
Macaroni and stewed tomatoes
Deviled eggs, scrambled eggs
Pinto beans
Onions
Head lettuce
Cabbage; sauerkraut; pickles
Apples, bananas
Pies: fruit, custard, lemon, pecan; fruit fried pies
In winter: canned green beans, beets, corn, peaches, tomatoes
    (some commercial, some home-canned)

In growing season: tomatoes, green beans, ear corn, spring
onions, radishes, okra, squash, new potatoes, beets/beet
greens, peaches, apricots, melons, pecans (usually Frieda
had a garden)
Hershey chocolate bars

My mother and grandmother made a big fuss about my eating when I
was a child. I hated milk. They bought boxes of flavor packets—cherry,
strawberry, banana, chocolate—and they cajoled me into drinking a glass
of milk after school. I liked macaroni and potatoes and beans. I ate canned
green beans and corn and fresh corn in summer. I'd eat a few bites of white
chicken; I liked to nibble the fat around a pork chop. I loved spaghetti and
meatballs and canned ChiliMac. A favorite sweet snack was iced graham
crackers. I would always eat toast. We never had a toaster; toast was prepared under the broiler (for cinnamon toast) or by frying slices of buttered
bread in a skillet.

Sometimes I wonder how I grew up on what I ate. I was a thin girl; really I was quite slender until I was forty or so. I learned to eat better when
I lived in California in my twenties: the fruits and vegetables were such
beautiful mounds of color in the grocery stores, and I learned to steam or
stir-fry. Once I married and had a child, I learned plain cooking, a sort of
healthier version of my grandmother's, with olive oil, fresh vegetables, and
a range of seasoning unheard of in the fifties—curry, cumin, chiles, fresh
Italian herbs, etc. I excelled at crepes, but otherwise have never mastered
desserts; my husband is a great pie maker. A couple times a year I make
lemon pie, using my aunt's recipe.

The older my husband and I got, just the two of us to feed, the fussier
we became about quality and the more I experimented with ethnic dishes.

Lately I don't care so much about food, though I try to make a nice supper, something simple and tasty. My husband eats breakfast; I don't. He eats leftovers, which pleases me. He eats apples and nuts for lunch. He fasts two days a week. He is healthy, vigorous, and wants to stay that way as long as he can.

I don't have his faith in food. I crave starches: beans, pasta with canned tomatoes, potatoes any way at all. I like pickles, coleslaw. I have a sweet tooth. I love Coke. I wish I could have one more apricot fried pie made with my grandmother's fruit.

I noticed by her late sixties that Frieda had severe indigestion. Sometimes she would stop, put her hand on her chest, and wait for her misery to pass. She ate tiny meals. Since my late forties, I have suffered the same ailment, which is a lot of the reason I don't take much pleasure in food anymore. I used to have terrible esophageal spasms (like angina), but there are medicines now to prevent that scary pain. She would be surprised to see how some common ailments don't have to plague you anymore. She would be happy that I can do something about a migraine when it hits.

The last year of her life, she didn't eat much of anything other than mashed potatoes. They were easy to make, easy to chew, easy to digest. I can see her point. She didn't really want to eat anymore; nothing in her needed feeding.

STARRY NIGHT

They were knock-offs, the popular paint-by-numbers kits, but Degas' *Dancers* and Van Gogh's *Starry Night* on the covers of the boxes thrilled me. Frieda bought them for my mother during her last illness, something she could do in bed. Each kit had a rolled-up canvas imprinted with the outlined image of a famous painting, and it was divided into a kind of diagram of hundreds of small spaces, each numbered to correspond with one of the small pots of paint that came in the kit. Mother had always liked to draw and had done some simple paintings of the Blessed Virgin Mary and one of me as a baby, but she didn't have the energy anymore to sketch or write or read.

Mother didn't ever work on the pictures, but years later, after college, I lived with Frieda for a year in her house in Wichita Falls, and I found the Degas canvas rolled up in her bedroom closet. I spent months patiently filling in the spaces. At first it made me cry, and then it became soothing, like knitting. I started the Van Gogh picture, too, although I don't think I ever finished it. Instead I brought home a book of impressionist paintings from the library at the Catholic high school where I was teaching, and I did sketches with an ink pen and quick splashes of watercolor. Paris street scenes were my favorite subject. I wrapped a few pictures in Saran Wrap, and years later they came back to me in my grandmother's things after her death. The plastic wrap had worked just fine to protect the watercolors.

Frieda started her painting lessons in 1960, during the year after my mother died, when she and I were living in a rented house in Odessa. I was in my senior year of high school, and she was studying nursing at the junior college. She met with a few other women on Saturday mornings in the teacher's home. They bought stretched canvases and painted from photographs or simple still life set-ups. It was hardly a classic approach to studying painting, but I realize now that Frieda learned a lot, and she had a natural facility for drawing, like Edith did. She never said what prompted her to take up art. I had a small painting Edith had done of the Blessed Virgin, and I propped it on my dresser in the bedroom. I remember Frieda saying it was too bad Edith never had a chance to take lessons.

Frieda continued studying with a teacher when she moved back to Wichita Falls. When I lived with her again in 1964 and 1965, I was surprised to see how serious she was about her painting. She constructed her own frames from purchased parts and stained or gilded them. She was good with color, and her brushstrokes were confident, though predictable. I can tell that she painted with a kind of precise determination, putting a stroke down exactly where she wanted it rather than brushing back and forth the way so many beginners do.

Her painting of a vase of sunflowers hangs on the wall across from me as I write this. She painted it from life, evident in its vividness and the lovely turns of the flowers. I look at it every day and think of her. Upstairs I have one of her still lifes, done with a muted ("grayed") palette, unlike any other of her paintings. It was stored for many years in my aunt's garage, so it needs cleaning. I plan to do it myself, as soon as I finish writing this manuscript about her. I love the idea of tenderly wiping away the dirty layer, letting the true colors appear.

I wonder if she minded that we all paid so little attention to her "hobby." Maybe I just didn't know what to say to her. That year I lived with her and taught, I was more interested than I had been in high school, and I liked to see what she had done in her class, what she brought home. She did a large landscape that year. Only now, when I paint landscapes myself, do I realize how much skill she had developed, to render water, trees, the muted distant ground. She tried to do her best, to get better; and if painting didn't bring her happiness, exactly, there must surely have been satisfaction in her accomplishment, and in the company. She was very patient; it took months to do a large painting; she only worked on it at her teacher's studio. Her landscapes were copied from calendars; I'm sure she never painted outdoors. She would surely have been amazed to see me with my painting gear, my sun hat and water bottle and apron, standing on a hill below Sienna, in Tuscany, trying to lay out the beautiful expanse of hills on my canvas. More amazing, I suppose, would be that I had the money to pay for something so frivolous in a place so far away.

One weekend she set up her table easel and a still life—a vase, flowers, and fruit on a table draped with a scarf—-and she told me I should give it a try. I remember spending the whole day, totally engrossed, and thrilled when I had covered my canvas with creamy paint. I used colors straight from the tube, without any mixing. I had no idea what I was doing, but it was fun. We celebrated by going out to Luby's Cafeteria for dinner. I never did any kind of art again until I was sixty years old.

My painting from 1965 took a circuitous route through back bedrooms and a cousin's house and finally to my basement, where my painting materials are kept. I like having it there near me while I am laying out my palette for a painting. I paint in my living room.

I started by painting an orange, and then a banana, and then smooth and rounded hills, like furred fruit. I haven't had a teacher, but I have looked at a lot of great art over many years, especially at the Metropolitan Museum in New York, and I learned from books. My daughter studied in New York and Philadelphia art schools, and a close friend is a painter; they have given me encouragement and gentle advice. From the beginning I was determined not to worry about how good my paintings were, even as I tried to learn skills. Often I do the same painting over and over again, sometimes on new supports, sometimes one on top of the first and another over that. Early on I had what I can only describe as a feeling about what I wanted to do—an aesthetic, I suppose—and I try to achieve it as well as I can. I sketch and do color studies and brood a while, and then I—just—paint. There is joy for me in the absence of words. The silence and concentration and the repetition—of strokes, shapes, whole paintings—are like a kind of walking meditation. The soft shush of the brush on linen. The faint odor of linseed oil. The ache in my knuckles.

I am deliberate, until I am not, and then I arrive at my painting.

My aunt and I have sometimes talked about Frieda's paintings. Not so much about the objects themselves or their quality as the fact that she had that impulse in her. She was so hardworking, so modest, so thrifty— the painting practice was a surprise because it opened a tiny crack in her secret self. I wish I could go back and tell her how much I admire her for her steady, patient study and practice; how glad I am that she was able to ease her pain, and moreover, to feed the drive she had to create beauty. I wish I could ask her how she got so good with her greens; maybe her teachers told her something she could pass on to me. Of course what I am wishing for is a chance to improve the quality of my time with her—to honestly share something with her that was important to her, something about which she had deep feelings. If only, I think; in other words, I wish I could feel better.

Whether she wanted approval or admiration is anybody's guess. She gave paintings to all of us kids directly or labeled some to be given away later. She gave me a landscape that was later stolen from my home (along with my antique doorknobs). There were a few paintings in her house when she died, and my aunt spirited them away into the trunk of her car, well before anybody started thinking about distribution.

I believe Frieda was proud of her painting. But mostly, I believe she did it for its own sake, immersing herself for those hours in the wordless, seductive sensuality of handling paint and the pleasure of watching an image emerge from her efforts. I think she painted because she loved it, and because it put her heart at rest, even if only for a while. I want the same things myself, now.

I recently read an article about a New York City artist, Janet Ruttenberg, who for fifteen years has been making huge paintings in Sheep Meadow, a section of New York's beautiful Central Park. She has never sold a single one, never tried, never wanted to. At eighty-two, she is finally showing the paintings in the Museum of the City of New York, because someone asked her if she would. She never wanted shows or sales. She just wanted to be out there, whole days at a time, in a place she loves.

I don't think Frieda reached that particular kind of pleasure. She didn't seem to care so much *what* she painted as that she painted at all. In a different life—one with the money for leisure and study—perhaps Frieda would have found a subject. A passion. She could have painted at her mother's farm in Devol, Oklahoma—the flat stretch of fields, the cobalt sky. Of course I'm projecting. I see what I am doing. It's not that I want her to have accomplished more, it's that I want her to have stepped out of her real life into one that appeals to me. I want her to have been happy in a way I can understand and embrace for myself.

She stopped abruptly. She put the paints and brushes away. I'm not sure when that was. It may have been because she suddenly had to care for her mother. Daddy Hill, her stepfather, and Tillie, her mother, had stayed on their farm in Devol into their eighties. Then Tillie had the first of several small strokes. Daddy Hill was frail, too, a thin man who had labored hard his whole life. There simply was no way for the couple to stay in the old farmhouse, though they feebly resisted moving, saying they wanted to die in their beds. Frieda understood their wish; she might even have wished it was possible to care for them at the farm. But they were living in another century, where water had to be carried in from a tank in the yard, on a derelict farm a significant drive away from stores. The heat in summer was intolerable. Water had to be heated on the stove to wash. And Tillie was increasingly childlike, frail and confused.

Frieda took her mother to her home, and her half-sister Frances took her father to hers. I wondered about the old couple being separated after more than half a century of marriage, but I could see that splitting them up was practical. Frieda would never have let Tillie be with anyone else, and her small house could not have accommodated two invalids.

I don't think Tillie and Daddy Hill ever saw one another again after the move. She might have forgotten him as her memories receded. She crinkled and faded, not, I think, in pain. I saw her once in that last year of her life, and, pleased to see me, she called me Edith. She took all of Frieda's attention. Frieda was ever so gentle, crooning to her mother, who slept on a rented hospital bed in the living room. Trained as a nurse and devoted to her mother, Frieda administered what we now call "palliative care." She kept her mother up part of the day, settling her in a chair where the light from a window would fall on her. She held her so that she could take a few steps. She held her when she whimpered in moments of feeling lost and weak. She rubbed her arms and buttocks with lotion. And in the night, she got up to shift her weight on the bed to prevent sores. That time I visited, I watched Frieda admiringly, thinking that there was so much love in her care for her mother. Frieda caught my gaze and looked at me with narrowed eyes. She said, nobody is going to have to take care of me. Don't even think about it.

Once she told me, out of the blue, that she had never spoken disrespectfully to her mother. We didn't use to do that in our family, she said.

I lay in bed later thinking about what she had said. Did she mean to scold me? I didn't think I had ever spoken to her in a bad way, either. I had glared. I certainly had pouted, but we had never actually quarreled. Maybe she had in mind the times her mother had criticized her or refused her help when she needed it and the fact that no matter what, Tillie was her mother, and Frieda had acknowledged that with respect. Now she was glad that she could look back and say that, because her mother had suffered in her life and kept working, serving, loving the best way she could, and Frieda would never have to wish she had been a better daughter. Maybe Frieda felt she herself had not been given due and loving consideration in her own life; maybe she held in her memory all sorts of harsh words shot at her, words that riddled her with regret.

What was she thinking of, then? Her son's tirades? My sullenness?

Mother's sharp remarks? The backtalk of young kids these days? Was she wishing she could say of us all, they always spoke to me with respect?

Tillie died, and shortly after, unexpectedly, Frieda's little sister Frances died suddenly of cancer, and Frieda took her stepfather into her home. He was a stick figure in his faded overalls. His voice was so hoarse and faint you couldn't understand him if he spoke, so he didn't try. She had never felt close to him, but she thought it was her duty to care for him. I think she might have drawn upon her training to find the patient neutrality that quelled her resentments. (He had never let her forget she wasn't his child. He had never done anything to make Tillie's life easier. He only cared about Frances. And on and on.) Only when he became too frail for her to manage did she put him in an elders' residence. She felt guilty, thinking of him feeling cast aside. But when she went to visit him, she discovered that the home was full of old farmers. Daddy Hill had brightened up. There was so much to talk about: old storms and droughts, failed crops and bountiful ones, turkeys—the dumbest of all animals—and pigs—smarter than you think; there were dominos. He had a good year, and then he faded fast, like a light dimming.

The last time I saw him, he was still in Frieda's home. I thought he looked apprehensive. Of course I didn't say that to her; what I did say was that he must be very grateful for what she was doing for him. Frieda said he would take a long time to die because he was afraid. In death he would finally be judged. Aren't we all? she asked, but I was sure she did not want an answer. I wondered if she got satisfaction from thinking of her stepfather pleading for entry into heaven. I wondered if she believed in heaven at all.

Recently my husband and I visited Paris, for all the usual reasons. On our last day, we took the train to Auvers-sur-Oise, the lovely village where Vincent Van Gogh spent his last seventy days, and where he and his brother, Theo, are buried. I had recently read a biography of the artist, and I felt awe and pity and love for him. He had tried to become a preacher, and failed;

then he turned to his true vocation, the way he was meant to honor God. His death had come as he was poised to join the mainstream of successful artists—some have said death catapulted him into fame. I do not believe that he was a suicide; I believe it is his work, not his myth, that makes him beloved, and I mourn the loss of what he might have done. The luminescence around the stars in his paintings may not have manifested happiness in his life, but I think it did manifest his joy in nature—and in painting.

It was a long walk uphill to the graveyard on the edge of the village. Standing with my back to the cemetery entrance, I looked out on an expanse of fields, imagining them golden with wheat, the way Van Gogh painted them. The graves are marked with two simple stones. In front of them, there is a small square plot of ivy. The wall of the cemetery is a foot or so behind the stones. I stepped alongside the plot and put my hands flat against the wall and shut my eyes for a moment. As I then stepped away, I saw a scrap of paper behind Vincent's stone, and I reached down to take it away. It was damp and rotting, but I could make out the faded writing on it: *You were holy and God loved you.*

I put the paper back.

Neither my mother nor my grandmother ever set foot in an art museum. If they ever saw a real painting, it would have been in a courthouse or library or church. But something in them craved to make art. Something in me does, too. I just want to pass the hours without words, without dreading judgment. I love cleaning my brushes.

THE SKILLET

The summer after my senior year at the University of Texas in Austin—I was short six credits for graduation—I rented a tiny studio in the back of an old couple's house. I could sit on my couch bed and stretch out my legs and touch the oven door. My grandmother drove down the weekend I moved in and brought me a lamp, sheets, and a few pots and pans. She pointed out to me that the cast-iron skillet had been my mother's and that it was well seasoned. You can fry eggs in it, she said. Bake cornbread.

Six weeks later, after my algebra final, I left Austin and went to New York on the train. I took a small suitcase of clothes and abandoned everything else. I knew I had done fine on my algebra final that morning, so there was one course done. I still had to do a semester of French, but not right then; I wanted to get out of Texas.

A year later I went to Austin again and completed my French requirement and graduated. Then I went to Wichita Falls.

One day I was going to fry potatoes. I pulled a skillet out of the drawer at the bottom of the stove. Frieda came into the kitchen and said, that's your mother's skillet, you know? There was a moment of silence, and then I answered in a whimper: from Austin? In a flash I knew exactly what had happened. She had given her phone number to my landlady that day she brought me provisions, and the woman had called her to tell her how abruptly I left, before my rent was even up. Frieda drove down to get what I had left behind.

I set the skillet on a burner and bent my head. Sorry, I muttered. And she laughed. God love her, she laughed and shook her head, waved her hand over her head like she was swatting flies, and walked away.

I'd say that was the closest thing to a reprimand I ever got from her.

THE GIRLS

She had friends. I was surprised, living with her as a young adult while I taught in a Catholic school, to notice her life in this particular way. I had only thought of her in relation to family. I didn't know very much about friendship. I didn't think about how close she had been to her painting teacher in Odessa the year after my mother died or to the women in her nursing program, who sometimes studied with her at our kitchen table and who endured with her the long night shifts at the hospital. She didn't have dates; she didn't dress up and go out. What were friends for? I thought. I wished I had some.

The phone rang almost every evening, and though I knew no one in Wichita Falls except the Sisters at school and my students, I ran to answer it. A woman would ask for my grandmother, usually by her last name: "Is Hambleton home?" The phone was on a chest in the hallway, and Frieda could take it into her bedroom on its long cord and shut the door.

They called one another by their last names; they called one another "the girls." She worked with them at General Mills packing flour, many of them for twenty years. She was shop steward that year, and there was always talk of union business. There was talk of how they were treated at the mill and whether they could do something about it. Some of the calls were to catch up on daytime soap operas. The girls worked rotating shifts, and those on days counted on the night shift girls to fill them in. Frieda had watched *As the World Turns* since its first season, and she didn't like to lose the thread of the story. She thought the brittle character Lisa Miller ought to get her comeuppance.

There was gossip, too. The girls had opinions about each other's problems. Every once in a while I'd hear Frieda laugh hard, from the belly, and I'd just about die, wanting to ask her what was so funny, but I never did. I thought I wouldn't understand old lady humor. Frieda was fifty-eight that year.

Sometimes the caller would ask me how it was going for me at school. I never failed to be surprised, caught at a loss for words. Fine, I'd say. There wasn't much else I could say about speech and English classes, sweet Catholic girls, the earnest, endless, good days I spent in the same building where I had been a grade school student and where I had lived as a boarder in seventh and eighth grade.

I was treading water, buoyed but out of sight of the shore.

A few times a year some of the girls from the mill got together at a restaurant. I went once, and it seemed to me all they did was talk about the food and weather. Another time that same year she met other graduates from Devol, Oklahoma High School at the same restaurant, and once again I went along. They were women who had played basketball with her, and I couldn't have told you how one group differed from the other, except that the Devol group mourned someone's death, and the ones from the mill looked stronger, harder, and wore pants and shirts instead of dresses.

Other than that, I don't think Frieda went out with anyone, but when you see the same people five days a week, talk to them at lunch and breaks, and then catch up by phone with the ones you missed, and you do this for years on end, you get close. I heard about one of the girls who had to have part of her colon removed, and another whose son had a car accident that was his fault. I met the women at the mill when I took supper to Frieda on many of the nights she worked a swing shift. (They were impressed that I did that. I used the trays frozen Mexican dinners had come in, but I cooked her something from scratch.) Of course I was young and shy and self-centered, and they seemed all the same to me, but I knew they were interested in me because they loved my grandmother. I was proud of her that they cared. And in some way, I was shy in the presence of their labor: their stringy, muscled arms, the sheen of flour on their faces and the wraps around their hair, their hunger and rushed eating. Their toughness awed me and made me feel small.

A few summers before she died, she came to see me in Oregon for the last time. We took her to the desert and to the coast. We took her on a canoe ride. When we met her plane, I was excited and on the edge of tears. I had had a bad year, not working, worrying about money and who I was, though I had a good life with my husband and daughter in small-town southern Oregon. The truth was, I spent too much time by myself.

Waiting for her arrival in the airport, I inched my way toward the front of the crowd. I spotted her right away as the plane unloaded. She came in the door holding her pocketbook across her chest like a child, and I watched her walk toward me. She was wearing a navy blue knit pants suit and a pink blouse and glasses that looked vaguely from the 1950s, with upturned corners, and her hair, which had always been curly, was soft and fine and flat against her skull. Below her pocketbook, I could see her belly pouch. I was shocked at the sight of her. She was old (seventy-five). It was the hair, I realized right away, that shocked me most.

I like your hair, I said, though I did not. She seemed fragile without the spring in her hair. It wasn't very gray, though.

The girl who always permed it for me died, she said. I didn't have the energy to make a new friend. I remembered that she went to the same woman month after month, year after year. She went to beauticians in their homes—women who had deep sinks in their kitchen or perhaps a plumbed porch off the living room and a chair with a big dryer where an easy chair might once have been. I'd gone with her a dozen times and read my book or dozed, bored to death, while they caught up on news of their families and talked about the weather.

A few days before Frieda was going back to Texas, I sat with her on the couch, my legs curled up under me, leaning against her. It had been raining all day, and the sun had just come out, and we talked about how nice that was, and I began to cry, to blubber, really, saying that I wished she would stay longer. I said I wished she wouldn't go back at all. Why did she need to live in Wichita Falls? She didn't have good neighbors anymore. She hardly left her house. Couldn't she stay with me? We could make a quilt, I suggested.

Are you so lonesome? she asked, and I nodded vigorously, as if I really could make her stay. She patted my hand. She said, you need to get out and make some friends. I was startled to realize that she wasn't lonely for me. It hurt my feelings for a long time, until I reminded myself that when I left home—and I mean the whole state of Texas—and all my kin within it, I lost my claim to loyalty. I had had a baby die, and later, his father died too; I had lost jobs and gotten married again; I had reasons for shame and for pride, but what I didn't have was that family, except for my grandmother. I didn't get Christmas cards or sympathy calls or invitations. I might as well have moved to Latvia.

Not long before he died, the writer and editor William Maxwell gave an interview on public television that I was fortunate to watch. He had been recently widowed, and when he was asked about the changes that had come to him in his very old age, he said that most of all, he didn't care much about the past anymore.

I thought then, and I think now, even more, that that might be the gift of old age, a kind of amnesia one doesn't fight. I hope it came to my grandmother—she didn't talk to me much in the last months; she didn't seem available to me anymore—and I hope it comes to me. I wonder if the very long labor of this book is part of that letting go. Don't we hold someone we love extra close when we say goodbye?

In the last summer, when Frieda knew her heart was going to fail her again, she retreated into isolation, as if her Grant Street house was an island washed by a boundless sea. She wanted nothing from any of us. I know there is a dream, a fantasy, of the "good death": the family around the bed, the soft light of a lamp, the muted fading away. I don't think many people die like that, and it doesn't make me sad that Frieda did not. She didn't want us there in her business. Nobody had anything she wanted. She had nothing more to give. No one could help her or accompany her. She had her own ideas about the end. She had her own way to go.

FRIEDA'S LAST HOUSE: 1953–1983

My grandmother moved into her new house on Grant Street in 1953. The lot was north of Midwestern Parkway and west of Kemp Boulevard, two major arteries of the city. At that time, it was one of the last houses on the street, though the prairie was already gridded for future construction.

She had been living in a small two-bedroom yellow stucco house at the north end of town, on North Lamar, a block off of what is now North Scott Avenue, south of Old Iowa Park Highway. It had been built in 1934, and it is still there. She had rented that house in January 1943, when she came to town from Gallup, New Mexico, to go to work packing flour for the Wichita Falls General Mill & Flour Co. In 1946 she was able to buy it for $2,400. It was perched above an unpaved street that flooded every spring. There were no sidewalks, and only a bare dirt driveway. The neighborhood was a village, with a one-block park and a small grocery store. The elementary school was Huey School. There was a bus a few blocks away that took her downtown, where she transferred to go out Kell Boulevard to the mill. Years later I would take that bus to Catholic school.

She had good neighbors. The greengrocer next door had two daughters, the same ages as my sister and I. Their mother, Ruby, was an age between my mother and my grandmother, so both women felt close to her. I think Frieda must have missed her when she moved.

The new house would be a much shorter drive to the mill, closer to shopping, and Frieda thought it would be a nicer house for her family as well as for her. It wasn't far from Midwestern University, and in later years she mentioned the possibility of renting a room to a student, but she never did. I attended school at Midwestern two different summers in the early sixties, but went full time in Austin. For the life of me, I can't remember why I didn't live with her and go to Midwestern, which would have made the most sense, financially and emotionally. At the University of Texas, I was desperately lonesome, a tiny, timid fish in much too large a pond. I know she would have liked for me to live with her, but she didn't press me. She never stated her preferences about my behavior, nor did she complain when my choices baffled her or hurt her feelings. I went away, and when I returned, we picked up as if nothing had ever come between us. Usually I called her for money to get home. I did tell her, when I was in my thirties, that I was sorry I had been so thoughtless. Saying it sent me into a fit of sobbing so that she had to comfort me, and my apology ended up being about me more than her, but I am glad I said something, however late and little.

She was friendly for a long time with a woman across Grant Street who was killed at her church on "Terrible Tuesday," 1979, when a record-breaking tornado devastated the city. (Frieda, meanwhile, was safe in the woman's storm cellar.) The new tenant of the house became friendly with Frieda too and was the person who found her dead in September 1983.

When she made the move across the city, Frieda couldn't have known that most of her neighbors through the years would be noisy renters with rogue dogs; that the street would become a detour for trucks; that two bad husbands would live in it, and her mother would die there; that the living room would be ruined twice, first by a flood, then by a fire caused by her wall gas heater. No one would ever really appreciate the house except her.

The house was an optimistic gesture, but also a shrewd one. A simple wooden box, it was better than the old house, but in no way grand. There were no sidewalks on the street. There was no real driveway. The house had small payments she could afford even if she were to be temporarily unemployed. The two bedrooms were cramped and the bathroom was tiny. The main room was quite narrow. There was no place for a washer and dryer. The water heater was so small that you could not take a hot bath right after doing dishes. In the kitchen, if four people crowded around the table, they blocked the door into the living room, and someone's shoulder was perilously close to the stove. In practice, if we were more than two, we ate on our laps, sitting here and there throughout the house. We slept on the spare bed, a couch, a camping cot, and a pallet in the hallway by the bathroom door. There was always room for family in her house. She knew what it was to be without a home, without resources.

In her life, neediness had been an indignity; now she owned a house where she would not be put out and she would not turn anyone away.

My mother, daddy, sister, and I were living with her on North Lamar at the time she built the Grant Street house, and I went with her on a series of many Saturdays to watch the house's progress. I thought it was bleak out there on the edge of the city, but new was new, and I expected to live in the house, so I found it exciting to see the changes, week to week. Once or twice a man she knew met us there, carrying brown bottles in a paper sack, walking the periphery of the large lot, drinking and making grumbly comments that I never quite caught. Once I saw him on a ladder. He was muttering angrily and pounding something with his fist, and Frieda told him, hush, there's a child here. He was nobody to me.

The two apricot trees Frieda planted in her backyard would bear fruit year after year. She stewed the apricots and made wonderful fried pies. She ordered rose bushes from Jackson & Perkins in Medford, Oregon, to plant in the front of the house, and they were there until her mother died and she began to let things go. After she moved in, she dug a garden and tended it for years, harvesting green onions, okra, tomatoes, snap beans, cantaloupe. She never cultivated a lawn. The huge backyard was weedy and peppered with stickers, except for the garden and the area near the back of the house, which was barren. The front of the lot had scant grass that ran out like spilled water, without a distinct border.

On those Saturdays with me on Grant Street, Frieda was uncharacteristically talkative. We walked about the lot, and took mincing steps inside the laid-out rooms, and sometimes we sat in her car, looking at the lot, as if the house might sprout while we were watching. We ate hamburgers bought at a nearby stand. She talked about her grandparents, with whom she and her mother and brothers had lived in Oklahoma after her father died in a farming accident when she was a little girl. They had been kind German farmers who seldom raised their voices and did not believe in striking children.

Frieda told me that her grandfather wouldn't let the boys shoot a bird. He said that farmers know that birds look after the land. He taught her to fish, a diversion she loved all of her life, and he taught her some songs in German, away from her mother, who didn't want her to speak the old tongue. I remember exactly her saying, they were so good and so dear. I know she meant her grandparents, but at the time I thought she meant the birds and the fish.

Her grandmother braided her hair and taught her to make bread and looked after Frieda while her mother went off the farm to clean houses in town. Now I think that must be how Frieda learned the special sweetness that can exist between the old and the young, something she took for granted as a child's right and gave as freely as a spring gives water. She was not a happy woman, but I got the best of her. I remember sitting in her car at the Grant Street lot, touching the soft flesh of her upper arm, and once, gently testing the skin along the jaw where it came up under her earlobes. She was skinny and sinewy, like a woman in a Dorothea Lange photograph, but she had a dapple of cushion in odd places, like fat stored for hard winters.

Later, when I would visit her on Grant Street, if I said I was hungry, she would drive two miles to buy me a corn dog if I wanted. She stocked canned ChiliMac and black cherry soda pop because they were my favorites. I never remember asking, can I have this? Can I have that? She never insisted that I eat what she ate, or clean my plate, or eat at certain times. She made special treats for us children, like graham crackers frosted with colored icing and frozen "pops" from Kool-Aid. She would give me her fried pork chop so that I could nibble the crispy fat off all around, and then she took it back to eat the meat, which I did not like. We ate brown beans ladled into bowls on crusty cornbread and she picked the salt pork out of mine. When I went to boarding school, she mailed me packages of fudge and cookies and tucked in a new pair of underwear. She was still mailing me packages the year she died, always seeing something she thought I could use.

When I think of "home," I think of my grandmother's house on Grant Street, the only stable real estate in my family history other than her step-father's farm in Devol, Oklahoma. Though my family did not move into the new house when it was completed, it was a constant in my life, the place whose pull I felt the most.

On a little shelf above the TV she kept a photograph of my mother and a silly wooden moose trinket she had bought in Lawton, Oklahoma, when we went to the mountains to swim and stay overnight in a rented cabin. I wanted to ask her if it was the same time we had to move out in the middle of the night because we discovered bed bugs, but I thought it would embarrass her, so I didn't bring it up. When I stayed with her, we watched late night TV—Jack Paar, including the night he cried and left the show, and then Johnny Carson.

She died in her house in September 1983. She was quite stubborn about spending her last months there alone. She had had bypass surgery in May in Lubbock, but it wasn't worth the torture. She went home and slowly tidied her house and life, paying off her son's last loan, planning who should get what pieces of furniture, cutting quilt blocks from old children's clothes. The neighbor across the street checked in on her after supper every evening and was in touch with Aunt Mae. Mae begged her mother to come back to Lubbock, but Frieda would have none of it. She didn't want any more medical attention. Nobody was going to put her in intensive care, plug her up to machines, and turn her into a bag of bones. There's a time to die.

She hardly spoke to any of us when we called that summer. I would phone and tell her things about my little girl and about how I had lost my teaching job because they said they couldn't afford a teacher with an advanced degree in a primary classroom. She would say, *well*. She was out of words. She hurt my feelings, sounding like she didn't want to talk to me anymore. I told my husband it was hardly worth calling, and then I went on long drives alone, rehearsing being without her. Once I stopped at a fence and shouted at sheep, What do you care! You never knew her!

My aunt and I were inconsolable for a long time, and the worst of it was thinking about Frieda alone in her house, but in time—years, really—we came to see that she died exactly as she wanted, with no one able to interfere. She was never an invalid, never dependent, never feeble. No one had to make any decisions for her or about her. Still, I was obsessed with thoughts of her last day for a long time. I conflated her death with a flood she had had in the house years before and imagined her on her kitchen table, waiting for help. I imagined her falling to the floor as one falls through ocean depths. I told myself a thousand times that she died fast and did not lie waiting, though in truth nobody ever gave me any details. Nothing helped but time. Now I think I understand her better. I've begun my eighth decade, and I know I wouldn't want painful intervention to prolong life either. I know I'll be thinking, thinking, right up until I die, and I'm trying to get used to the idea that I'll take everything unsaid with me. That used to scare me, but now there's comfort in the notion of privacy in death, and of the shedding of all burden.

OPAL ON DRY GROUND

Whatever I feel about my grandmother—her life, her death—I don't forget that she was Mae's mother. My aunt's loss haunts me and compounds my own. In my fourth novel, a character, Opal, has not recovered from her mother's recent death. In the excerpt of the novel below, she dreams about her mother's death, a dream that is my own.

The novel is about Opal and her two daughters, whose lives are in sorry flux. I didn't know that Opal's fierce commitment to her daughters sprang from her own relationship with her mother until I wrote about her. I didn't know that I would write the dream until I did. What is true, what is felt, what is imagined; what you want, what you feel, what you mourn; these things are the sinew of fiction.

She dreams.

She sees herself at a table, perched on a hill like a bird at a feeder. The barren hill floats between sky and water. She dials a phone again and again. There are no edges to the dream.

She sees her mother. Greta is in her house, making her bed with new sheets. She shakes them out and smooths the creases. The sheets billow above the bed and float down slowly. The sheets have a pattern of roses. Rain splashes on the windowpane. Greta crawls on the bed, between the flowered sheets.

"Did you think you would die in your sleep?" Opal asks in her dream, but Greta does not hear. "Were you afraid?" she asks in Greta's ear, and a current washes her away. "Mama!" she calls, swimming helplessly against the current.

The roses swell and drift, then settle again over Greta, a comforter of roses. She sleeps, she wakes. She goes around the house, turning on the gas heaters. For a moment, she is clear and present and real, and even in sleep, Opal's heart aches.

From her hill, Opal sees the house, across the water. The rain pours; waves splash against the foundation of the house. The house rocks slowly.

Greta opens the front door and steps out onto the tiny concrete porch.

"Careful!" Opal cries. Her mother is both near and far—the house is *over there* and yet her mother seems close enough to touch. Opal puts out her hand, but her mother is out of reach. Opal is both inside and outside the dream, inside and outside her mother's house. She understands that it is a dream, and she draws back her arm, not to interrupt, not to wake up and lose her mother. She retreats, to save the dream.

Greta peers out over the lake of the yard. There is a man at the edge of her lot. "Who are you?" she yells. The man shouts back, "Help is coming, don't be alarmed."

"Go inside!" Opal calls.

"Go inside!" the man calls. He sloshes closer. "Get up on the table," he tells her. "You can float."

She closes the door with a thump. Water is seeping in, her feet are wet. She takes off her shoes and socks and dries her feet carefully, especially gentle across the corns. She puts on a heavy sweater. Each movement is liquid; her very edges are watery. She takes a quilt off the bed. She goes to the kitchen and opens her quilt on the table and climbs on top. "Dear God," she prays. She hugs her knees.

Water laps in the kitchen.

* * *

"Mama, Mama," Opal cries. She dials and dials.

The table is a raft. Greta seems to drift in the loss of light.

"Hold on!" Opal cries, as if the dream is another chance, as if she does not know it is a dream, it is too late.

The water rises in the kitchen, stranding Greta on the table. She pulls the quilt tight around her. She gargles gravel bubbles nobody is around to hear, then crumples. She slips like polished stone, mile and miles toward the green linoleum, the ocean floor.

ADMONITIONS

Wear deodorant.
Don't pout.
Eat the leftovers.
Hang up your dress. And your towel.
Clean up your messes.
Keep your hair clean. Make a straight part.
Bite your tongue.
Answer your elders. Don't sass.
Stop biting your nails.
Turn off lights.
Fill up the tank before you need to.
Rinse your dish.
Don't complain: If you can't have it, if you don't want to, if it
    isn't fair.
When you're bored, keep it to yourself.
Don't let a stranger know that you're upset.
Get out of the way.
Don't gossip. Don't say anything you'd mind having repeated.
Don't be nosy.
Don't beg when the answer is no.
Don't let boys tell you dirty jokes.
Study and practice. God made you smart for a reason.
Write thank you notes.
Be polite to clerks and cleaners and everyone who labors. Be
    wary of salesmen.
Keep the tub, the toilet, the sinks, and the kitchen floor clean.

Don't envy rich people. You have what you need, and they're
no better than you.
Take care of your belongings. A lot of things will last a lifetime.
Look out for the little kids.
Remember I love you.

IRA WRITES

ra was a sociable man; he liked jokes, he teased her, he liked to talk day or night. He still had a boy's mischief in him. Once when they were living in Gallup over a summer, when Frieda's brother Lou found work for him, they went on a drive, the four of them—Lou, Ira, the wives. They were on the reservation and Frieda said, Watch where you drive, they won't like it, you know. It's their land.

But someone had told Ira the Navajos were dancing, and he thought it would be a wonderful thing to see. He had an idea about where to go. Lou parked, and the men went on, walking, while the women stayed in the car, stubborn and nervous. Ira told them, we'll keep our distance.

Oh, the two of them, Lou's wife said, but Frieda heard what she really meant: That Ira!

Along a little rise, they walked low, and then crawled, excited to see that Ira was right—the Natives were dressed up, beating drums, yelling, and dancing. The two men were so enthralled they didn't even notice the approach of men behind them until they were snatched from their hunched positions and shoved and scooted down the incline, right into the midst of the hollering Indians.

And then who danced? The Natives called out for the men to empty their pockets, and with much hooting came the command to jump! Dance! After a while they laughed and pounded Lou and Ira on their backs and sent them on their way.

No harm done, except of course the loss of the wallets. Ira couldn't stop laughing. By golly, didn't he dance with the Indians?

The wives were furious. Think of what could have happened!

They had no money to lose, did they? And yet it was gone.

* * *

Eula Mae heard the story after Ira died. She was ten years old. Her mother was sick with anger and grief. Out of nowhere, she started talking. Ira, always home late because he had one more joke to hear or tell. Ira, eating supper one bean at a time on his fork, pretending he wasn't hungry, grinning at Frieda, smacking his lips.

Mae was such a little girl, to hear that her father was a fool. He was jerked off the back of a pickup truck, and his head pounded into the highway by a whirlwind. After the funeral, Frieda said: He should have been up against the truck cab, like all the others. He was probably showing off, his legs dangling at the end of the truck bed like a man with his toes in a pond. He was a fool, a man who danced with Indians, and then got in the way of a whirlwind, when all of us need him so much, when we won't be able to make it without him.

IRA WRITES: SWEETHEART

Grand Canyon, Arizona
October 4, 1934

Sweetheart,

You are a dear I think the world of you an those sweet baby's. It sure is hard to stay here, but as hard as times are an no money makes one do it.

The more I see of the wemon an Girls here running around the more I Love you dear. I know you are true and some day I am going to be back with you an be happy.

Honey you may not mean so much to them but you are the world to me. I wish I could put my arm's around you an try to sooth your heartacks, but as I can't I send my Love an kisses in this letter to the dearist little mother in the world.

Your Ira

CREDITS

"Under the Apricot Tree" appeared in *America: The National Catholic Review*.

Part of "Anger" appeared in *Image*.

"Leave-taking" appeared in *Women on the North American Plains* under a different title.

A portion of *Mysteries of Love and Grief* was published in *Narrative* magazine.

Excerpts were from the novels *Opal on Dry Ground* and *Plain Seeing*, both by Sandra Scofield.

"Frieda's Larder" first appeared as "My Grandmother's Larder" in *Southern Women's Review*.

Mysteries of Love and Grief is Texas Tech University Press's second Judith Keeling Book.

The Judith Keeling Book, established in recognition of a lifetime of achievement in and dedication to scholarly publishing, honors books that are undertaken through careful research and assiduous attention to detail, that investigate questions posed by any inquiring mind, and that make a valuable, perhaps otherwise unnoticed, contribution to the scholarly community and to the literary culture of Texas and the American West.